Malcolm Johnson · February

SEEN IN BRITAIN

SEEN IN BRITAIN

Henry Pluckrose

Mills & Boon Ltd
London · Sydney · Toronto

First published in Great Britain 1977
by Mills & Boon Limited,
17–19 Foley Street,
London W1A 1DR.

© Mills & Boon Ltd. 1977

ISBN 0 263 06294 5

Book designed by Alec Davis.

Filmset and Printed in Great Britain
by Thomson Litho Ltd., East Kilbride,
Scotland.

Acknowledgements

Photographs by Henry Pluckrose,
Warren Farnworth and Margaret
Slack, photographs and drawings by
Alec Davis, and drawings by Chris
Evans, Tony Matthews, Christine
Robins, Nigel Chamberlain and
Christopher Floyd.

The publishers are grateful to the
following for permission to
reproduce illustrations:

Aerofilms Ltd, 206; Belgrave Hall
Museum, Leicester, 52; Bignor
Roman Villa, 57; British Museum
Trustees, 10, 26; British Rail, London
Midland Region, 166, 167; British
Waterways Board, 183; Cambridge
University Museum of Archaeology
and Ethnology, 26; Camera Press
Ltd, 174; Central Electricity
Generating Board, 201; City of
Birmingham Museums and Art
Gallery, 26; Clive Coote, 30–34;
Henry Grant, 221; Keystone Press
Agency Ltd, 221; Borough of
Blackburn Recreation Department,
27; Manchester City Planning
Committee and Derek Lovejoy &
Partners, 175; Trevor Matthews, 92,
93; Hugh McKnight, 176, 179, 182;
Milk Marketing Board, 103; Museum
of British Transport, 158, 169;
Museum of English Rural Life,
University of Reading, 106; Museum
of Leathercraft, 26; Museum of
London, 22; National Coal Board,
32; National Railway Museum, 160,
161; Norwich City Council, 22;
Nottingham Museum and Art Gallery,
27; Port of London Authority, 198;
Public Record Office and Museum,
12; Science Museum, London, 27,
159, 160, 161 (Crown Copyright);
James H. Smith, 90, 91, 93; Southern
Newspapers Ltd, 89; Victoria and
Albert Museum, 27 (Crown
Copyright); Tom Viney; 89; Wallace
Collection, 96.

Contents

ABOUT BRITAIN

The one date which everybody
remembers from their school history
lessons is 1066—the year in
which William, Duke of Normandy,
landed near Hastings and defeated
the Saxon King, Harold Godwinson.
This proved to be the final invasion
of Britain. Celt and Roman, Jute,
Saxon and Dane had, in earlier
centuries, settled here. Each race
brought a culture of its own which
intermingled over the years with
those already there.

But the year 1066 *was* special. Never
again would a foreign army
determine the character and
development of the British people.
Wars there would certainly be—
between Lancaster and York,
Roundhead and Cavalier, Stuart and
Hanover, Englishman and native
Scot—but such changes in
Government as were made were the
result of the clash of domestic
factions and not a result of foreign
intervention.

Thus for over nine hundred years
Britain has developed without
suffering the cataclysmic changes
which can follow defeat in war.
Unlike the Low Countries, the British
Isles has never become the
battleground of warring armies;
unlike the people of Palestine, the
people of Britain have never seen
their homeland disintegrate under
the conflicting demands of rival
political and ethnic groups.

Continuity in the pattern of daily life
has been a characteristic of the
British. Indeed, even William I
stressed that his aim would be to
respect the customs and practices of

Edward the Confessor. He came to
build on the past not to destroy it.
The Domesday Book was his way
of ensuring that the traditional
economic responsibilities of Lord
and serf, and the customs and
practices which confirmed them,
would not easily be forgotten.

A nation which can develop in
this way is fortunate. Customs are
preserved from one generation to
the next to illuminate our
understanding and appreciation of
the past. Wells are still dressed with
flowers in many Derbyshire villages,
even though most of the cottages
now receive piped water. This
practice serves to remind us of our
dependence upon water, and also of
those magical stories of our
childhood when woods were
peopled with fairy folk, spirits and
water gods. Since The Green Man,
Robin Goodfellow, Puck and Robin
Hood lived in the minds of our
ancestors, as well as in their songs

and stories, it's not in the least
surprising to find that the little man
of the woods still peers at us through
the carvings at Southwell Cathedral
as well as from many a sign on a
village pub. Both brewer and cleric
came to terms with the folk culture
they served!

Our customs also live on through
people. Her Majesty, for example,
still receives 'quit rents' in the most
unlikely commodities, such as like
roses and nails. Despite the mass
media each new Lord Mayor of
London trundles across the city
every November in an uncomfortable
coach so that the citizens can 'see
his face'. An unknown Lord Mayor
would be unable to command
respect should the gates be
threatened—and *then* what might
happen?

But it's not only through traditional
customs that our heritage is passed
from one generation to the next.

Freedom from foreign armies has meant that much of our man-made environment has also been preserved. Such battles as were fought involved comparatively small armies. With the exception of Cumberland's rape of Scotland, following the rising of 1745, the warring armies did not regard themselves as alien to the people over whose lands they fought. Thus although towns were occasionally burnt and castles slighted, damage through war has been superficial. Cromwell's soldiers did not attempt to destroy Royalist castles completely. They were required only to weaken their defences, so as to make prolonged defence impossible in a future engagement. The same principle seems to have been applied to cathedrals and churches. Statues were vandalised and the tombs were used to sharpen swords—but if the roof kept out the rain, and the Lady Chapel could be used to house pigs and horses, it seemed unnecessary to destroy the structure. Of course the fire bombs and high explosives which were dropped upon cities in World War II had their effect. Some city centres were virtually destroyed. Such is the wealth of our historic past, however, that the loss today is hardly noticeable.

Continuity in government, a legal system which down the ages has emphasised the place of property in society, together with a church which patronised the Arts, provided the framework in which craftsmen could flourish.

But British craftsmen were also fortunate in that there was a plentiful supply of material on which they could work. Stone as varied in type as granite, limestone and marble; wood from lime and oak; iron and clay—all these resources meant that houses, palaces, cathedrals and castles could be built to last.

To the skill of their native born craftsmen must be added the readiness of the British to adapt ideas and practices which had been successful on the continent. They were made relevant to local requirements and incorporated with local methods and styles. Thus the impregnable fortresses built across Wales by Edward I owed far more to Crusader and Turk than to a revolution in British military thought. Similarly the change in the style of domestic buildings in the 17th

century must be attributed to the Huguenots, who settled in England rather than suffer persecution for their religious beliefs at the hands of French Catholics. Their influence can be seen at its strongest in Eastern England, where red-bricked gabled houses relate far more closely to Bruges than to Birmingham or Bolton.

These combined factors—a country rich in natural resources, a settled population, a hybrid people full of diverse skills, together with a temperate climate—have left Britain richer in artefacts than almost any other nation in Europe. Many British roads, for instance, owe their origin to Roman colonists. Some like Peddars Way in East Anglia, follow tracks laid down centuries before the Legions by Celtic farmers and traders. Some roads take us along routes once followed by the

mediaeval wagoner, others along the macadamed roadways of the nineteenth century stage coach.

But along all of these roads, be they motorway or village lane, there remains evidence of our past. Buildings, memorials, inscriptions, statues, place names and street furniture remind us of things that were. We can, of course, speed by and never notice. We can look and not see. We can be so wrapped up in the present that we fail to appreciate the past which surrounds us. We so often pass by when we ought to stop, hurry when we ought to wander, concentrate on road signs when we ought to find time to stop and wonder at spires and the fall of ancient roof tops.

Even though we think we know a place there remain odd things to discover, curiosities to unravel, however commonplace and everyday they may seem—the coal hole covers you tread on as you walk to work, patterns in the brickwork of the local railway station, the names of streets. It is often possible to look at familiar things in a new way, to see everyday things for the first time.

It is also possible to relate past to present. The universal appeal of History is that, being human, we can appreciate the problems which were faced and overcome by human beings who lived long ago. The dilemma of Thomas More—should political expediency over-ride individual belief—is one which applies to our age as much as to Tudor England. Childbirth, marriage

and death, law and order, economic growth and decay, the problems posed by disease, poverty and religious difference have been common to mankind since the beginning of time. It is salutary to remember that just as these 'modern' problems are not new, neither are the environmental decisions which we are continually called upon to make. All the buildings we see around us were once modern. An eighteenth century corner cottage may have been built over someone's walk to work or

destroyed a view that someone in the past took for granted. The route of Brunel's railroad, the line of the Bridgewater canal, the position of the city wall at Canterbury, the siting of the castle at Edinburgh were all planned at some stage in our history and, to some extent, have continuously influenced and affected the lives of the people who have lived in their shadow.

Perhaps it is as well that we look to this aspect of our heritage, to understand that decisions which we make today can affect the life style of generations yet unborn. It's not just that we should romance over our past. It's not that we should sentimentalise over things old and refuse to accept technological innovation. Rather, we should consider the implications of developments in our cities and across our countryside.

It's pointless writing letters to *The Times*, the local council and departments of state when the motorway has arrived, the power station has been built or the town centre destroyed for redevelopment. By then, it's too late.

LONDON

'He who is tired of London,' remarked Dr Johnson, 'is tired of life.' Life, of course, is the one thing that London has never been lacking. Indeed, Dr Johnson's observation could be applied to almost any period of London's history. Today, though much of the city that our grandparents knew has disappeared, sufficient remains to remind us of the past.

Nobody really knows when London was born. The Thames certainly helped its growth, for rivers carry boats and boats carry people and goods. Some historians believe that the British King Cunobelin (the Cymbeline of Shakespeare) had a port on the north bank of the river to serve his town of Verulam (the Verulamium of the Romans). The name London certainly suggests a Celtic root—Llyn (or Lin) meaning 'pool' and din (or deen) a 'fortified place'. But whoever was responsible for its original foundation, we know from Tacitus (who lived between 55–120 AD) that Londonium was 'crowned with traders and a great centre of commerce'.

Its importance in these early years is illustrated by its defences—built after Boudicca and her Iceni tribesmen had ravaged the city in 61 AD. The great wall, which was over 6 metres high and 2.5 metres thick, enclosed 135 hectares and gave protection to the Bridge which was to play such a prominent part in London's development.

The story of London is far-ranging and complex, and the casual visitor would be advised to concentrate upon those things which are of particular interest to him. The new Museum of London would be an excellent place to begin—for here, interests, once identified, can be followed with visits to places in the city. Ecclesiastic interests are readily served, for in addition to four cathedrals, London has a wealth of old churches. Norman and Mediaeval buildings are as common as those of Wren and Nash.

London abounds in 'royal' connections, from the Changing of the Guard at Buckingham Palace to the palaces of St. James, Eltham, Kensington and Westminister (where Parliament now sits); from the trooping of the colour to the Queen's house at Greenwich and Tudor Hampton Court.

London's artistic heritage is immense, for as well as being rich in galleries it is also rich in museums which house the mementoes and bric-à-brac of famous people. Their lives are recorded by statue, road name and council plaque ... and some far less conventionally: Christopher Wren's memorial is St. Paul's; Thomas Gresham's is a grasshopper; Eros is a tribute to Lord Shaftesbury.

We can also learn much of London through its river. The Thames from Hampton Court to Tilbury has played a very real part in the City's life, political and commercial. Across the Thames the citizens fled with their possessions during the Great Fire; down the Thames to Traitors' Gate went Elizabeth Tudor; along the Thames have gone state barge and lighterman's tug, passenger wherry and oil tanker, passenger liner and collier. Nowadays the port is much quieter than it once was and the dockland from the Pool to Greenwich is being redeveloped. But ships are still to be found— HMS *Belfast*, HMS *Wellington*, *The Cutty Sark*, Chichester's *Gypsy Moth* and Scott's *Discovery*— reminders of a maritime past.

Contemporary interests can also be satisfied. When the Great Fire wiped out much of the old city it was rebuilt in a fashion which probably caused some Londoners to make rather rude remarks about 'modern buildings' ... remarks no doubt similar to those made today about new office blocks. But continual rebirth is what keeps a city alive. What is pleasant about London is that the new has never quite managed to obliterate the old. Contrasting styles touch each other and somehow blend. This quality applies not only to its buildings but also to its method of government.

Dr Johnson would undoubtedly find modern London totally unrecognisable, but in its own way, just as fascinating as the city he knew.

ROMAN LONDON

This head of Mithras, the mysterious
Persian sun-god, was found in
the remains of a Roman temple.

Sections of the Roman wall of
London still stand as evidence of
Roman settlement. Here, at Cooper's
Row, the base is Roman.

Mosaics, like this one from a
larger frieze, decorated the houses
of the rich, and public buildings.

SAXONS ...

A scramasax—a dagger carried by the fierce invaders from northern Europe—in the Tower of London.

Carved stone cross from All Hallows Berkying-by-the-Tower where the remains provide evidence of life in Saxon times.

The shrine in Westminster Abbey of Edward the Confessor, last of the true Saxon kings. Parts of the Saxon Abbey can be seen in the passage to the Little Cloister and the bases of some pillars.

The remains of a seventh-century arch, probably the oldest in London, at All Hallows'.

- Abacus
- Chamfer
- Capital (Simple cushion)
- Pier, shaft or column
- Base
- Plinth

Norman architecture was called 'Romanesque' and was characterised by pillars like these.

Round arches, St. John's Chapel, Tower of London.

...AND NORMANS

William the Conqueror built the Tower of London on the Thames to protect the land and river approaches to London.

An example of beautiful Norman architecture is St Bartholomew the Great, Smithfield. The oriel window was added later.

Old London Bridge, which took thirty-three years to build and lasted six hundred years, was the only bridge crossing the Thames until 1749.

The Domesday Book (1086) recorded the land holdings and feudal responsibilities of every member of Norman society.

12

MEDIAEVAL LONDON

A Maltese cross—white on black—the badge of the Hospitallers of St John.

Edward I had a coronation chair made in 1301 to contain the famous Stone of Scone. It is in Westminster Abbey where it has been used for coronations for almost seven hundred years.

The Guildhall has been the centre of government for the City of London for over a thousand years. The Lord Mayor always belongs to a city gild, or 'Livery Company'.

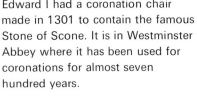

London street names give clues to trades of the past. In Lombard Street, named after the Italian bankers, banks still retain their hanging signs.

TUDOR LONDON

The Tudor rose, symbol of King Henry VII and the Tudors.

Banners of the Knights of the Order of the Bath are hung in the Henry VII Chapel, Westminister Abbey. When a new knight is created his banner is hung up.

Hampton Court Palace, built by Cardinal Wolsey, was given to Henry VIII.

Shakespeare's famous Globe Theatre was built in Southwark.

THE STUARTS

The Great Fire of London, 1666,
is commemorated by the
Monument. Most of the old city
was destroyed. London's skyline
changed under the Stuarts. St Paul's
cathedral was rebuilt by Sir
Christopher Wren. His new churches,
like St Bride's, often had steeples.

Inigo Jones built
Queen's House
in Greenwich.
It is now part
of the National
Maritime Museum.

GEORGIAN & REGENCY

Georgian London reflects the classical influence of Southern Europe with its rows of terraces. Here at 48 Doughty Street, Charles Dickens lived. Architects such as Kent and Adam planned attractive interiors. The level of eighteenth century craftsmanship was very high.

Increased trade was created by the growing Empire and brought wealth to London's merchants who built houses, squares and crescents in the West End. Church Row, Hampstead is one of the finest examples of a Georgian street still existing in London.

St Mary-le-Strand, built at the order of Queen Anne.

The lions on Westminster Bridge are made of 'Coade', an artificial stone.

The National Gallery, Trafalgar Square was built by William Wilkins, and contains a magnificent art collection.

VICTORIAN TIMES

The Law Courts (*above*) were designed by G E Street (1874) in mediaeval style complete with towers and turrets.

Westminster Cathedral exemplifies Victorian revivalist architecture with its decorated brickwork.

The Albert Memorial and Albert Hall were built by Queen Victoria to commemorate Prince Albert, her husband.

Palm House, Kew, is iron, steel and glass.

MODERN LONDON

The Royal Festival Hall, Queen Elizabeth Hall, the Hayward Gallery, the National Film Theatre and the New National Theatre are all part of the modern South Bank complex.

Millbank Tower stands 118 metres high and dwarfs the recently extended Tate Gallery.

The Post Office Tower, built in 1965, is the tallest building in Britain. It is 175 metres high. Modern methods have made building on London's soft clay possible.

URBAN LIVING

We tend to think of the development of the town as a comparatively modern phenomenon. But this is not the case. The very word 'town' betrays its Anglo-Saxon root, for 'tun' meant 'homestead' or 'place of shelter'—which is what a town came to be. In times of unrest towns were fortresses; but they were also market places, places where roads met and often places where a river could be crossed or where there was a good harbour for sea-going ships. Their glamour attracted people, and continues to do so. They were places of work, industry and wealth. If they were somewhat unhygienic to live in, there were always plenty of people who were ready to risk disease for the excitement, pace and imagined riches of urban life.

Many British towns can trace their roots back to pre-Roman times— Colchester, York, Lincoln, Bath and Gloucester among them. The Romans built upon these population centres and founded towns of their own, some of which like Silchester and Wroxeter no longer exist. Although the Saxons did not favour urban life, Thetford, Ipswich, Stamford and Southampton date from this period in our history.

When the Normans came they introduced new techniques of government. The towns were strengthened. Military strength brought security, and security brought in its wake industry and trade. The citizens of towns, to show their special position in society, were given the title of 'burghers'. As they grew richer, the towns were able to bargain with the king. In exchange for grants of money, towns were granted certain 'liberties' such as limited self-government. Lincoln, Bury St Edmunds, Gloucester, Exeter, York. The Cinque Ports, Oxford, Winchester, Chester, Carlisle, Bristol, to list but a few, boasted royal charters which enabled them to hold fairs, appoint magistrates, mayors and aldermen; to control through its gilds labour regulations and the marketing of goods; to pass local law and, eventually, to send representatives to Parliament.

The old established charter towns such as those mentioned above are fascinating places to visit. At the centre are usually found the oldest buildings—merchants' houses (often converted to shops) facing each other down a wide central roadway which was once a mediaeval market place, or neatly grouped around a central square; the shirehall and the customs house; the parish church and the gildhall; alms house and gabled inn. Around this central core will be buildings which illustrate the town's gradual expansion—Tudor timber frame houses giving way to Jacobean brick, Jacobean giving way to Georgian, Georgian to Regency, Regency to Victorian, Victorian to Edwardian villa and the concrete, glass and steel of our own day. This concentric development has often been altered by generations of town planners and improvers, but for the person who wishes to look for the past this rule of thumb method of research has much to commend it.

Streets and their names will also throw some light upon the use to which particular parts of the town were once put ... names like Maddermarket (Norwich), Milk Street (Exeter), Cheapside (London), Mercers Row (Northampton), Cornmarket (Oxford), Horsefair Street and Haymarket (Leicester).

Not all towns are rooted so deeply in our past. Some towns, such as Buxton, Harrogate and Brighton, became fashionable as spas; others developed because of a new industrial process. Thus Sheffield is largely the product of the explosion in steel production in the 19th century, Stourport grew round a canal, Crewe around a railway. Some towns have grown around a University, others because a Government department has chosen a site for development or because a quixotic philanthropist decided to be remembered by an ideal factory and its associated 'people's housing'.

The effect of the changing pattern of transportation can also be seen in most town centres. The coaching inn remains—with cars instead of horses in the stables; the railway station, if one exists, will be found a little away from the market square—for trains were rarely brought right into town. This pattern is continued today, for airports have to be built away from population centres.

This changing pattern of urban life is preserved in many local museums and galleries. Maps and costumes, artefacts from home and factory, reports of borough surveyor and parish beadle all help us to relate things that were with things that are. At a time when it is becoming more and more difficult for us to preserve our environment as systematically as we ought, the local museum has the considerable responsibility of saving something of our urban past for future generations to enjoy.

SHOPS & MARKET PLACES

Many towns had a weekly market in Saxon times, mainly for the exchange of farm produce for town goods. A market cross, at first of wood, marked the spot where goods were brought and sold. Tradesmen paid a toll for the right to sell. As the market grew, the cross became a structure, sometimes with a room on top to house the weights and measures. This stone market cross was built in 1783 at Swaffham, Norfolk.

Street markets still flourish, such as Surrey Street Market in Croydon.

The local supermarket is a far cry from the old market cross, with goods in modern packaging from all over the world.

Helmsley Market, Yorkshire, is
constructed early in the morning.
while (*above right*) Bolton Market
Hall is a permanent, imposing
edifice.

A hypermarket, like this one at Telford, is a huge supermarket, catering
mainly for the motorist.

London Street, Norwich, was jammed with cars in 1966. Parking was difficult and shopping dangerous.

In 1967 the street was closed to traffic to create a pedestrian precinct, with the result that shopping became pleasant and traffic-free, much as it was back in the early 1850s.

This eighteenth century shop front can be seen at the Museum of London. Museums in York and Leeds, among others, also have old shops.

A modern shop front.

A lock-up shop can be shuttered and completely closed, like a box.

A kiosk is an outdoor stand.

A boutique, the French word for shop, often displays goods outside.

The Royal Arcade, Norwich, is grand in the *art nouveau* style, with pillars, glass and stonework.

SHOP DETAILS

stone frieze

slate roof

wooden upper facia

tile hung front

glass facia

metal window frames

marble stall-rising

Different building materials often appear in shop front design.

Brackets, pillars and capitals can make a most interesting study.

Shops which supply goods to Her Majesty the Queen are allowed to display the Royal Arms.

TEAS & ICES, CONFECTIONERY, CIGARETTES.

Look for signs with unusual wording, lettering and decorations.

Not surprisingly this modern sign advertises wines for sale.

Years ago a shopkeeper would hang out a sign to illustrate his trade for those who could not read. This old sign of the Peterboat and Doublet once hung outside a London rope and twine maker's shop.

The three gold balls of the pawnbroker were taken from the coat of arms of the Medici family.

The sheaf of corn remains where a bakery once thrived. The shop has changed but the old sign is a reminder of times past.

As well as a clock for the watchmaker, there was a key for the ironmonger and pestle and mortar for the chemist.

At the sign of the shears one would expect to find tailors and outfitters.

TOWN MUSEUMS

Silver: Communion cup with the
H mark of Kingston-upon-Hull
c. 1570–75, made by Peter Carlill,
Birmingham Museum.

China: The Wallace Collection has
examples of Sèvres and other ware.
This cup and saucer was softly
coloured—in London.

Clay: Neolithic beaker,
Museum of Archaeology,
Cambridge.

Stone: Flint tools are found in
museums in different parts of the
country.

Ivory: Piece from twelfth century
chess set, in the British Museum.

Horn: A child's horn book was
named after the transparent sheet
of horn placed over the text to
protect it.

Wood: This late medieval chest is
carved with Gothic tracery.

26

This late seventeenth century carriage is in the City of Nottingham Museum.

Greek coins can be seen in a number of museums.

A replica of James Hargreaves' 'Spinning Jenny' is shown in the Lewis Textile Museum, Blackburn.

An English gentleman doll of 1740 shows the dress of the period. The Victoria and Albert Museum, London, has a large collection of historic dolls.

This model of a Gloster, the first British jet-propelled aircraft, is displayed in the Science Museum, London.

INDUSTRY & POWER

This mill in Chelmsford, Essex, has what is called a lucam. This part of the building houses the hoisting gear, which raises the grain up into the storage loft, ready for grinding.

There are three main groups of watermills—

1   Overshot: the wheel is turned by the weight of water falling on to the paddles.
2   Pitchback: A version of the overshot.
3   Undershot: Turned by a flowing stream.
4   Breastshot: Water hits the wheel at breast height.

Old mill stones often survive when everything else at a mill has decayed.

The water (1) turns the wheel (2), the shaft on which the wheel is fixed (3) turns a large cog-wheel called a pit wheel (4). The pit wheel turns a wallower (5), which in turn passes power to the spur wheel (6) which turns the millstones (7) which grind the grain.

Smock mills were so called because they looked like the smocks worn by country people. Only the top (or cap) and sails can be moved. This is Upminster Smock Mill, Essex.

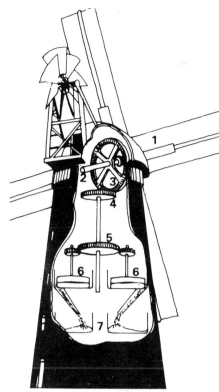

The workings of a windmill: sails (1); axle tree (2); brake wheel (3); wallflower (4); spur wheel (5); mill stones (6); meal bins (7). The windmill operates on the same principle as a watermill. The pit wheel is called a brake wheel, but apart from that the workings are the same.

A chute for passing out the sacks of ground grain.

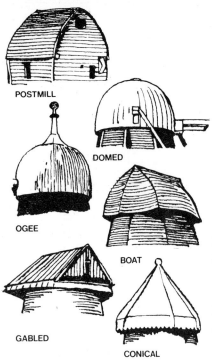

POSTMILL

DOMED

OGEE

BOAT

GABLED

CONICAL

The cap is the part that sits on top of a smock mill or tower mill, into which the sail axle is fitted. Caps are many different shapes.

Old structures often remain around disused mines. This is the preserved engine house at Elsecar in Yorkshire. Up until about 1800, most beam engines were used for pumping water from the mine. Later they were used for winding cages to carry men or ore up and down the shaft. One end of the beam engine lies inside the building, the other juts out over the disused shaft.

Post mill near Great Chishill in Cambridgeshire.

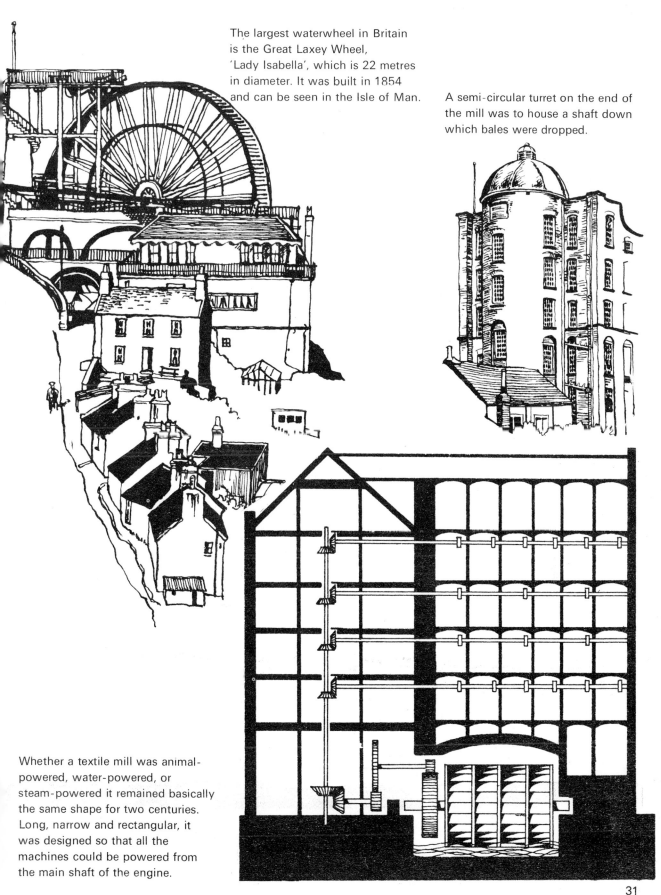

The largest waterwheel in Britain
is the Great Laxey Wheel,
'Lady Isabella', which is 22 metres
in diameter. It was built in 1854
and can be seen in the Isle of Man.

A semi-circular turret on the end of
the mill was to house a shaft down
which bales were dropped.

Whether a textile mill was animal-
powered, water-powered, or
steam-powered it remained basically
the same shape for two centuries.
Long, narrow and rectangular, it
was designed so that all the
machines could be powered from
the main shaft of the engine.

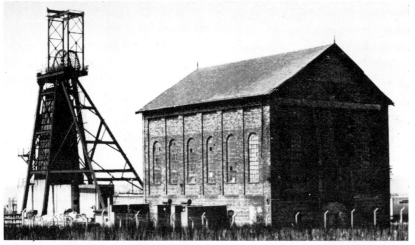

A large, brick-built engine house stands alongside an early twentieth century winding headgear. Steel cables connect the engine wheel in the engine house to the winding wheels on top of the headstock. From the headstock the cables drop vertically into the mine shaft.

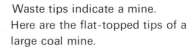

A miner's house in Blackhall, Durham, shows the time he had to be awakened for his shift.

Waste tips indicate a mine. Here are the flat-topped tips of a large coal mine.

An old furnace pond—well fenced-off.

A view of one of the bottle kilns
in the courtyard of the Gladstone
Pottery Museum, Langton,
Stoke-on-Trent.

These miners' houses are at
Wrexham in North Wales. The name
of the street, 'Colliery Road', shows
the connection with mining. Collier
is the old name for coal miner.

Solid brick industrial buildings often
have unexpected ornamentation.
Date plaques and original factory
names give clues to past uses.

A pub sign can give useful clues about the area's industry.

Lemington Glass Cone, Northumberland.

Iron-ore digger.

AIRPORTS

Passengers at an airport arrive at the terminal building.
A commemorative plaque at Terminal 1, Heathrow, London.

British Airways Trident jets being prepared for flight: at the rear,
refuelling is taking place and a catering truck is unloading; in the
foreground a baggage train unloads passengers' luggage.

The passengers board via covered ramps from the terminal.

Inside the terminal, passengers
check in and their baggage is taken
by conveyor belts to the aeroplane.
Modern, spherical loud speakers
are used to make flight
announcements throughout the
terminal.

Using radio and radar, the control tower oversees all movements on the airfield.

Powerful tractors are used to move an aeroplane from the apron, where it has been waiting, to the runway where it can use its own power.

A Boeing 747 'Jumbo Jet' ready for take off, destination Australia.

Some small airfields are for private flying. This is Dunstable Down in Bedfordshire, a centre for the popular sport of gliding. A tractor winch propels a glider into the air.

Disused RAF airfields make an interesting study, especially those used during the Battle of Britain.

ROADS

We live in an age dominated by the internal combustion engine. As motor technology has become more sophisticated our roads have had to cope with a rapidly increasing flow of traffic—faster cars, heavier lorries, bigger coaches. But our road network, which until the First World War was little more than a haphazard combination of village by-roads, wagoners' routes, mail coach and old toll roads, was quite inadequate to meet the new demands placed upon it. To accommodate the car and the lorry motorways have been built and trunk roads widened. Acres of farmland have been gobbled up in the process, harsh white concrete has replaced the subtle colours of the countryside ... such is the price of progress.

Watching the slow spread of motorway across the countryside might prompt the discerning reader to consider how the Romans ever managed to link London to Chester, York, Norwich, Dover, Exeter, Bath and Carlisle with straight well-drained highways. Indeed the Roman engineer—could he return to gaze at the vast range of equipment used by his modern counterpart—might be excused for observing that he marched his roads across wild countryside using nothing more than primitive tools and legionary manpower. It is

something of a compliment to the Roman builder to notice how often our modern roads follow his routes, or to ask whether any of our road surfaces will remain intact two thousand years from now—as intact, for example, as the Roman road to be found in the Forest of Dean near Blakeney.

It's easy, of course, to forget that there were roads long before the Romans. These early roads were little more than grassy trails, made and continuously preserved by the tread of countless travellers, their cattle and their horses, long before Roman engineers came to knit parts of them into the communication system of the Empire. The Icknield Way, which runs from Holme-next-the-Sea (Norfolk) to Wallingford (Oxfordshire); the Ridgeway, which links the Icknield Way with Avebury and Stonehenge; the Pilgrims Way, which joins Folkstone to Stonehenge; and the Jurassic Way, which stretches from Whitton (Lincolnshire) to Northampton are the most famous of these 'green roads'. On any long journey today's traveller will touch upon, cross, and perhaps even follow routes first established centuries ago. Thus a good road atlas, which shows past as well as present, is a necessity for any motorist who wants to explore as well as travel.

Because the function of the road remains unchanged, we can expect to find along its length echoes of our history. It is obvious, for example, that vehicles cannot cross wide rivers unless there is a bridge, a ferry or a ford. Many bridges which date back to mediaeval times now carry traffic loads undreamed of when they were constructed. General Wade's bridges, built to open up the Highlands to his English troops after the rising of 1745, are now used by tourists rather than troopers. The quaint rural toll bridge, designed to facilitate the passage of wagon and drover, still lives alongside its 20th century steel and concrete counterpart. Similarly the modern motel is a direct descendant of the post house where travellers rested between the stages of their coach journey. The blue and white route signs are a development of the humble mile stone and rural signpost. Sadly, some things have largely disappeared, to be seen occasionally as a quaint reminder of a less hurried age—oddly shaped toll houses on quiet unused roads; horse troughs where there are no longer horses; roadside crosses, memorials and village signs which recall customs and beliefs no longer widely practised; a lock up, pillory and stocks. Indeed the very names of the places through which the road runs often proclaim an industry, a craft or a person long since dead ... Monkscombe, Kersey, Edwinstowe, Abbess Roding, Chester, Street, Iron Acton, Saffron Walden.

'The world runs on wheels', wrote John Stowe in his *Survey of London*. The wheels now run faster and the very speed of their running may well result in our never really seeing the things we pass by. Perhaps we should remember that our roads not only carry us *between* but also *through*!

Roman roads cover the length and breadth of Britain and many of our modern roads follow their routes. They are generally very straight, linking a number of large towns such as York, Lincoln, Exeter, Bath, Leicester, Dover and Chichester with London. This stretch of road is in the Forest of Dean, Gloucestershire.

Before the days of tarmac and concrete, road surfaces were made from stones, sometimes quite large. Stones the same size are called setts and are often made of granite. More

irregular stones are called cobbles. In this Burford street a combination of setts and cobbles makes up the roadway.

Modern streets may show a tarmac surface, with stone curbing and a concrete pavement. They can be repaired easily, or dug-up without difficulty to get to various under-street services.

Villiers Street - Between Strand and Embankment

TYPES
OF ROADS

Roads have many names. This is the Victoria Embankment, London. An Embankment borders a river or railway.

A passage in Bath for pedestrians only.

Streets with 'cheap', 'chep', or 'chipping' in their names had markets once. Above is a broadway, Broad Street, Chipping Sodbury, Avon. Other towns might have a Market Street, or places with the word 'market' in them.

The miles of M5 Motorway provide a link from Exeter to Carlisle.

This narrow street in York is called the Shambles.

This mews is near Hyde Park Corner. A mews is where falcons were once kept.

A crescent was a specially planned street, as in this fine sweep of Georgian houses in Bath, Avon.

'Rotten Row' in Hyde Park is said to come from 'route du Roi', royal road.

Along steep streets houses may be built in terraces.

Cathedral Close, Gloucester, encloses the cathedral.

This avenue is tree-lined.

Houses were built around a square, as in Soho Square, London.

A causeway is a raised road across water or marshes.

Piccadilly Circus in London is a roundabout with Eros at its centre.

The mediaeval Rows at Chester are raised above street level and shoppers are separated from road traffic.

BRIDGES

A multi-arched mediaeval bridge at Bradford-on-Avon, Wiltshire, was built with a chapel for travellers.

This fourteenth century fortified gate straddles the road on the Monnow Bridge, Gwent.

A pack-horse bridge has bays where pedestrians could step aside at the approach of a cart, wagon or horses.

Bigsweir Bridge built by Telford is a single-span iron bridge over the River Wye.

On a turnpike road a toll was paid at the toll gate, like this on Bathampton Bridge, Avon.

Some bridges can be raised to allow ships to pass underneath. Here, traffic is held up while Tower Bridge is raised to let a ship into the Pool of London.

Modern construction has made possible roadway bridges of reinforced concrete such as this bridge on the M5 Motorway.

The Severn Bridge, a good example of a modern suspension bridge, links Wales and England by motorway. It was opened by the Queen in 1966. A toll is taken from all motorists who cross it. The income is used for its upkeep.

ON THE ROADSIDE

This milestone in West Wycombe, Buckinghamshire was erected by Sir Francis Dashwood to commemorate the completion of the road in 1752.

The Little Market House, called the Shambles or the Pepperpot, in High Wycombe, Buckinghamshire, was built in 1761 to a design by Robert Adam. It also serves as a signpost.

Road signs are designed to be easily understood, without words.

A finger-post made of cast iron at Farmington, Gloucestershire.

A stone cross serves as a finger-post at Eastlington, Gloucestershire.

Gantry signs, ones which span the road, are easy for motorists to read, and allow them to get into the lane they want as early as possible on a fast motorway.

An old Yorkshire milestone.

A milestone on the London—Oxford stagecoach route.

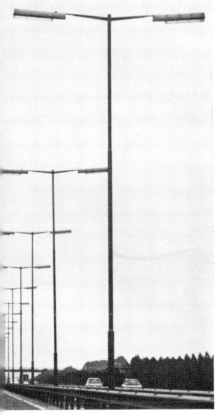

Lights on the M4 Motorway serve both sides of the road.

Lamplighters were people whose job it was to turn the gas lamps on and off. Some gas lamps have been converted to electricity while others have been replaced altogether. The old lamp posts tend to be made from ornate iron, while modern ones are fashioned from concrete or tubular metal.

Two Victorian pillar boxes plus one old one doubling as a milestone.

Former horse and cattle troughs can be put to decorative use.

A converted gas lamp with a dolphin at its base, Thames Embankment.

A cattle-grid, with bars set a few centimetres apart, prevents cows or sheep from straying.

INNS &
COACHING

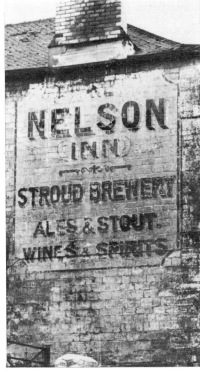

Some inns are now closed and converted to private houses, but clues like this painted sign remain.

The passage through which the coach was driven was called a porte-cochère and led to the courtyard.

A horse mounting block outside The Mermaid, Burford, Oxfordshire, shows signs of long and heavy wear.

A coach carried the mail.

Inn signs can be three dimensional, like this one at The Smugglers, Warren Street, London.

The inner courtyard of a fifteenth century coaching inn in Gloucester is galleried around the first floor.

This is the Beaumanor Coach (1740) with its leather suspension, at Belgrave Hall Museum, Leicester.

A coaching inn at Brockworth, Gloucestershire, has the name and sign of a once famous and fast type of coach.

Coaching inns are often very old and are built from local materials. Their signs often are coats of arms of the local lords or knights who once owned the land. A sign can illustrate aspects of the locality such as this one at Puesdown.

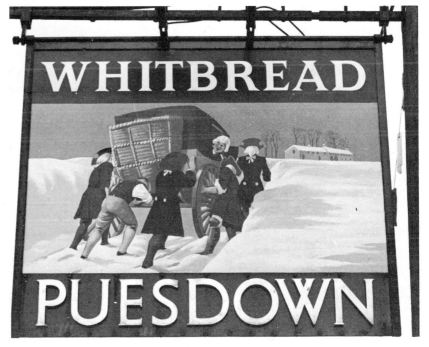

This house was once the staging post and stables of the Bow Street Runners. In the eighteenth century they formed the only detective force in and around the capital.

It is difficult for old roads to cope with modern traffic. This town gate in Chepstow, Gwent, is very narrow. A by-pass sometimes provides the answer to this problem.

In a small village or town there are many things to look for by the roadside. Statues, war memorials, old pumps or watering troughs, mounting blocks, as well as pillar boxes and street lamps are all worth noting. This cross in Malmesbury, Wiltshire, for instance, was built in 1490, and apparently was used during the Civil War to solemnize marriages.

HOUSES

The arrival of mass building techniques, which brought with it a rash of semi-detached bungalows, new Georgian town houses, planned estates and towerblocks, has blinded us, perhaps, to the real nature of domestic architecture in Britain. A modern, centrally heated house built in Leeds in 1977 looks much like a house built at the same time in many other towns. This is not surprising. The components used in the building will have been mass produced to a pre-determined design, from door frames to window lights, from water closets to kitchen fittings.

Fortunately this has not always been the case. The vernacular, or domestic, builders of the past usually depended upon materials that were locally available. This had the effect of first creating and then preserving an indigenous labour force skilled in the techniques necessary to shape and fashion local wood and stone.

Thus the character of an area is often illustrated by its older houses—the cruck houses of Herefordshire and Gloucestershire indicate counties once rich in well-established woodland; the cob houses of Devon and Dorset (built from a mixture of mud, chippings, straw and farmyard dung) show a dependence upon agriculture; the timber-faced dwellings of Essex and Kent indicate the availability of wood but little building stone. Similarly, the attractive limestone cottages which run in a swath across England from Wiltshire through Oxfordshire, Warwickshire, Worcestershire, Northamptonshire to Yorkshire, tell of a plentiful supply of cheap local stone. There are few timber houses in Cornwall, but many built of granite; few thatched cottages in the Highlands; we find dry stone walls in Dorset and Derbyshire; walls of flint and pebble in coastal Norfolk.

After identifying local characteristics, it is possible to look for specific details. Is brick used throughout the building (as in much of Lincolnshire) or simply as an infilling between timber beams (as in East Anglia)? If the house is faced with cob or plaster, is it highly decorated (as in Suffolk) or left smooth (as in Devon)? The roof will also indicate local tradition— grey slate, stone or ceramic tile, straw or reed thatch being used to complete the building and to give it harmony with its neighbours.

Windows and doors are also of interest. If the house was used as a place of work as well as a home, it is likely that its doors and windows will reflect the fact. If a house were used for weaving, for example, it would need good lighting. This might be indicated by windows high in the eaves. The weaver's houses of Golcar, Delph and Dobcross are typical of this development.

Alternatively the house might be extended to provide a work area at ground floor level. The village smithy is probably the most obvious example of this functional alteration of house design. However, many villages in the Midlands contain houses which were specifically designed so that their tenants could live alongside their machinery. The cottages of the stocking frame workers of Hathern (Leicestershire), for example, had an extension lit by a large window and heated by a central chimney stack. Even in winter the workroom would stay tolerably warm and light.

The style of window and doorway will to some extent reflect the period in which the house was built Glass, of course, is a comparatively recent innovation. The original window was a hole, a 'wind eye', which was nothing more than an opening so that the owner could see 'which way the wind was blowing'. A lattice of twigs, woven diagonally, covered the hole. This weave caused the rain to run downwards and outwards—thus preventing too many drips from falling inside the room. The lattice pattern was adapted by the early glass makers, who quickly moved to more efficient glazing techniques, which employed larger areas of glass and smaller quantities of lead. It is amusing to observe that this folk design was 'rediscovered' during the 1920s by architects who wished to add a touch of Tudor grandeur to their three bedroomed 'semis'.

Each house, however, though reflective of its time and the purpose for which it was built, is unique. The marks of individuals remain—a family marriage recalled by initials in the brickwork, a horse mounting stone beside a garage, a well or a pump in the garden, a snuffer for the link boy's taper set beside electric coach lights in the porch, a house anchor, a weather vane, an insurance plaque. Even the name of the house may tell us something.

THE DEVELOPMENT OF HOUSES

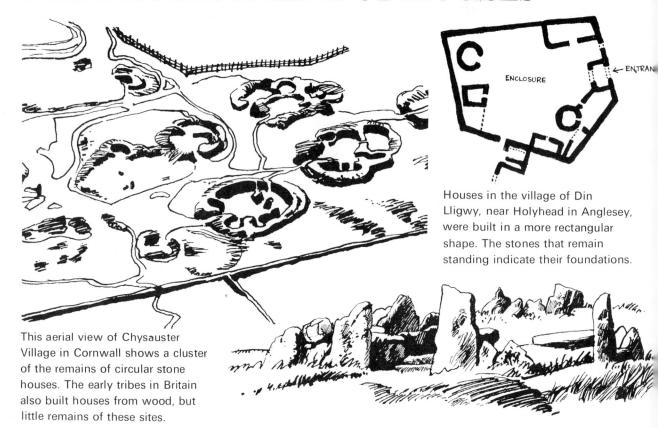

Houses in the village of Din Lligwy, near Holyhead in Anglesey, were built in a more rectangular shape. The stones that remain standing indicate their foundations.

This aerial view of Chysauster Village in Cornwall shows a cluster of the remains of circular stone houses. The early tribes in Britain also built houses from wood, but little remains of these sites.

A hut in the Neolithic village of Skara Brae in the Orkney Islands shows that furniture, the hearth and boxes to hold food and water, were all made of stone. The village had been buried in sand for thousands of years, thus preserving it.

The Romans cut and shaped stone and made and decorated their own tiles from clay. They used mosaics for beautiful decorations. They made water pipes from lead and leather, paved their courtyards, and made their houses comfortable. The Roman central heating was called a hypocaust as in this villa at Bignor in Sussex. Hot air flowed through the channels beneath the floor to give under-floor heating.

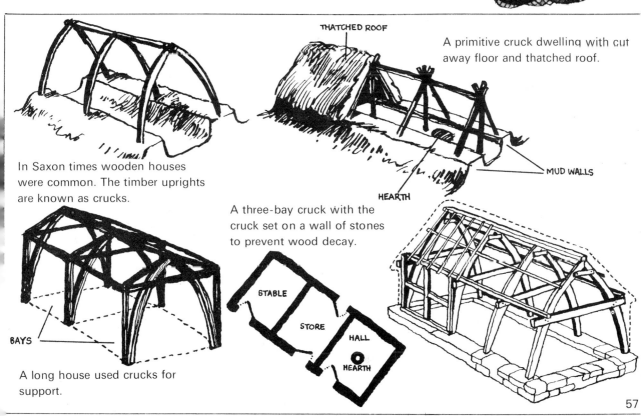

THATCHED ROOF

A primitive cruck dwelling with cut away floor and thatched roof.

In Saxon times wooden houses were common. The timber uprights are known as crucks.

MUD WALLS

HEARTH

A three-bay cruck with the cruck set on a wall of stones to prevent wood decay.

BAYS

STABLE

STORE

HALL

HEARTH

A long house used crucks for support.

57

A fourteenth century cruck cottage in Didbrook, Gloucestershire.

The crucks are still visible on the gable end of this house in Ledbury, Herefordshire.

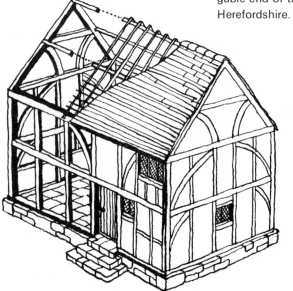

A timber box-framed house was the next stage in house development.

A stone chimney replaced the old smoke hole and could be added easily to the outside wall of a house.

Here the structure of a Suffolk frame house is shown during renovation. This style was practised until late Stuart times. Later buildings were more sophisticated.

A dormer set in the roof provides light in the upper storey.

All kinds of filling were used between beams. The framework could be filled with wattle and daub as shown here. Wattle panels were made from hazel stakes. After they were fixed in place they were filled with clay or cow dung mixed with straw or animal hair, and then whitewashed.

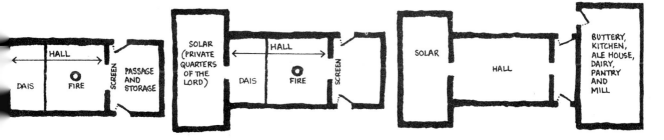

Most mediaeval villages had a manor house, built in stone or with timber framing.

The Lord's house might be developed like this.

An extension was provided for the servants. The hall was still the centre-piece of the house.

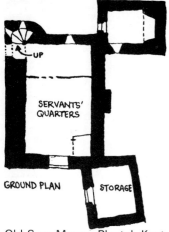

GROUND PLAN

Old Soar Manor, Plaxtol. Kent,
(c. 1290) is stone built on two
floors.

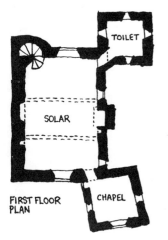

FIRST FLOOR
PLAN

It is similar to earlier houses
in basic design.

A photograph of Old Soar Manor today. Under the chapel is a room for
storage, and the room beneath the solar is the servants' quarters.

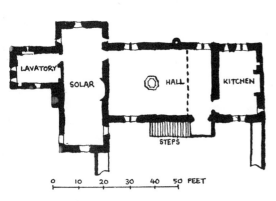

The design of a manor house
from the time of Edward I, c. 1300,
shows thought for defence.

This staircase may once have led to a door, now replaced by a window.

A moated manor house (c. 1340) at Ightham, Kent clearly shows the timber framework. The moat was good defence against attackers or intruders.

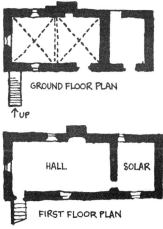

GROUND FLOOR PLAN

↑UP

HALL   SOLAR

FIRST FLOOR PLAN

Boothby Pagnell Manor, Lincolnshire, built c. 1180, has vaulted lower rooms which are used for storage. The living quarters were on the first floor, approached by an easily defended staircase.

The plan shows one of the most complete examples of a hall-house in Britain.

GROUND FLOOR PLAN

This manor house dates from the time of Richard III, c. 1480. In the plan the hall is still shown as an important feature.

The screen passage in Fir Tree Farm, Forncett St Mary, Norfolk, divides the kitchen from the hall. On the left is the doorway to the hall, on the right two doorways to the kitchen. In early Tudor halls the minstrels' gallery was situated over the screens.

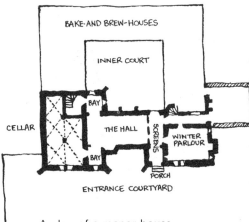

A plan of a manor house built about 1490 shows that the Great Hall is still central to the design but takes up a smaller proportion of the building than before.

This old farmhouse in Cumbria reflects the original style of the extended manor house. It contains an ancient courtroom.

In Lavenham, Suffolk, well-preserved mediaeval houses clearly show the wooden frame construction. The houses usually had a narrow frontage onto the road but were very deep.

Mediaeval townhouses were built upwards rather than outwards so that as many buildings as possible could be fitted within the town walls. The houses were jettied, as here at Abbot's Lodge in Ledbury, Herefordshire, which means that the upper floors overhung a smaller ground floor to give maximum living space. Along the backs of the houses there was often a narrow lane called row, close or back.

The Merchant's House in Yarmouth, Norfolk (c. 1600).

The Queen's House, Greenwich, was designed by Inigo Jones, who lived from 1573—1652.

Renaissance style houses such as this, in Lincoln's Inn Fields, London, reflect classical influences from Greece and Rome, which inspired the architects Inigo Jones and Christopher Wren.

Crewe House, Curzon Street, London, is a fine Georgian town house.

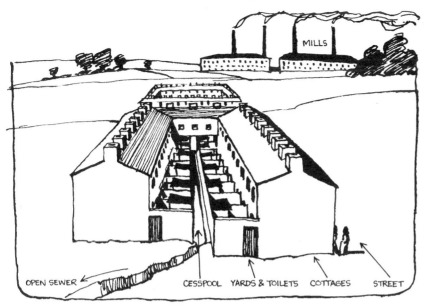

OPEN SEWER CESSPOOL YARDS & TOILETS COTTAGES STREET

In the nineteenth century the new factories needed men and women to work in them. Houses were built close together near the factories in order to house as many workers as possible. This drawing of houses in Preston, Lancashire, shows the cotton mill in the distance, and the back to back houses with their open drains and cramped conditions.

These industrial houses in Newcastle-upon-Tyne provide accommodation for two families, one up and one down. The doors are in pairs—one for each family.

Today whole areas of old houses may be torn down for the building of a new estate. This one is in London.

A Victorian house, built in the 1860s, shows a great variety of styles contained in one building.

OUTSIDE HOUSES-WALLS

Wooden timbering provides the basic structure in Tower Hill House in Bromyard, Herefordshire, dated 1630. It has varying lozenge designs. Wattle and daub was used for filling.

A plaster decoration known as pargeting on 'Cromwell's House', Saffron Walden, Essex.

In parts of south-east England timber facing known as weather-boarding, or clapboarding, was used, as on this house in Essex.

Brick infilling, called brick nogging, was sometimes used. Here, on a house in Lavenham, Suffolk, the pattern of the bricks is herringbone.

Tiles were made in a variety of patterns.

Some houses were faced with tile. Tile making had nearly disappeared during the thirteenth century, but was revived in 1784.

Stone was used for building in parts of England from about the year 650. One of the earliest stone-built dwellings in Europe is this one on Steep Hill, Lincoln.

The Tribunal, Glastonbury, Somerset, is built of large, regular-shaped stone.

Stone was often used in its natural rough form and not always cut to shape.

ENGLISH BONDING   FLEMISH BONDING

DIAMOND DIAPERING

When the Flemings settled in England in late Tudor times they introduced the bonding we use today. Bricks could also be used to give pattern to buildings.

ROOFS

HIPPED ROOF ALL SIDES SLOPING INWARDS.

HIPPED (MANSARD) ROOF – PERFECTED BY FRENCH ARCHITECT MANSARD (d. 1666), IT GAVE MORE SPACE IN THE ROOF AREA.

HIPPED M-SHAPED ROOF

GABLED ROOF ROOF SLOPING ON TWO FACING SIDES.

GABLED ROOF WITH CATSLIDE

HALF-HIPPED ROOF OR HIPPED GABLE

GABLED MANSARD ROOF

GABLED M-SHAPED ROOF

A stone roof in Worth Matravers, Dorset. The heaviest tiles were at the house walls.

Hand-made tiles can have a slight camber to them, for they warp in the kiln.

Pantiles overlap, providing channels for rain to run down.

Thatched roofs are found in most parts of Britain and are commonly made from reeds, rush, broom and heather, and straw from barley, wheat and rye. Here a thatcher is using a wooden 'bat' to drive home the Norfolk reeds. A large cottage may take about eight weeks to roof.

Interesting details can be seen on thatched houses. This one is near Corfe in Dorset.

A cottage in Denton, Northamptonshire shows a pattern of 'sways' at the apex of the roof.

A kneeler along the gable adds attractive detail.

A Dutch gable—more common where the Flemings settled.

Cow steps make an interesting decoration.

69

A thirteenth century chimney and a fourteenth century modelled chimney cover.

Seventeenth-century chimneys.

Carved oak bargeboarding was used to decorate this Sussex house.

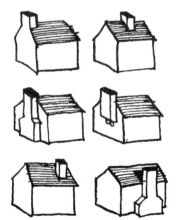

Chimneys can be placed in a number of different positions. If the fireplace is on the first floor the ground floor may have been used for animals or storage.

This pottery louvre or smoke vent (c.1300—25) fitted in the roof above the open hearth of a great hall.

Decorated Tudor brick chimney at Denver in Northamptonshire.

WINDOWS

EARLY ENGLISH

1400

TUDOR

TUDOR

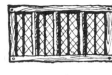

WOODEN MULLION

STONE FRAME WITH IRON BARS

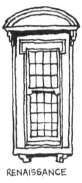

RENAISSANCE

GEORGIAN

REGENCY

QUEEN ANNE

A Tudor lattice window.

Seventeenth century windows on a manor house in Gloucestershire are surmounted by a 'dripstone'.

A 'Venetian' window.

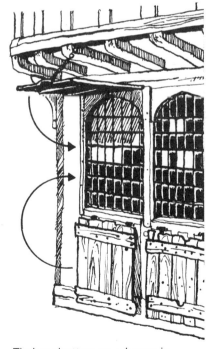

Timber shutters on a house in Lavenham, Suffolk, can cover the windows from the top and from the bottom.

71

In this late-eighteenth century London terrace the windows reduce in height with each additional storey.

A Queen Anne bow window in Maldon, Essex, reflects a number of other different window styles.

Windows on a box-framed weaver's cottage in Lavenham, Suffolk, are large in order to give extra working light.

DOORS

13TH CENTURY

1400-1470

TUDOR

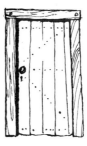

HEAVY WOOD FRAME

SUB-MEDIEVAL

TUDOR

RENAISSANCE

QUEEN ANNE

GEORGIAN

REGENCY
1800-20

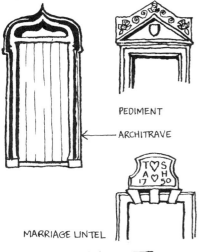

PEDIMENT

ARCHITRAVE

MARRIAGE LINTEL

A Queen Anne period window canopy shaped like a shell. Some were built over doors.

An old oak-panelled doorway in Lavenham, Suffolk.

A brick, sedan-chair porch in Chester, Cheshire. Wind porches date from 1550.

A plaque on a house may commemorate a famous person who once lived there, or may give the date when the house was built. This is a dated cottage in Nayland, Suffolk.

Above the trelliswork porch on this cottage in Denton, Cambridgeshire, is a date plaque.

Insurance marks date from the time when each large insurance company had its own fire brigade. This stamp is for a policy issued in 1742.

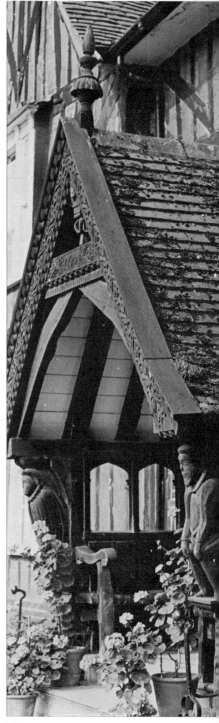

This seventeenth century wood and tile porch in Long Melford, Suffolk, is ornately carved and decorated.

A carved face peers from a wall in Fordham, Cambridge.

A coat of arms decorates a Tudor battlemented turret.

Houses may take unusual shapes and forms. This house near Lochearnhead, Tayside, has a round tower and spire.

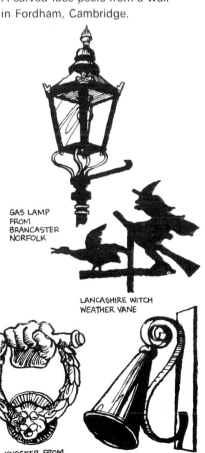

GAS LAMP FROM BRANCASTER NORFOLK

LANCASHIRE WITCH WEATHER VANE

KNOCKER FROM BATHAMPTON, SOMERSET

LINK SNUFFER, BATH, SOMERSET

A water pipe tells the trade of a house's owner: a master ship builder.

In Thaxted, Essex, a lead water pipe gives the date of the house.

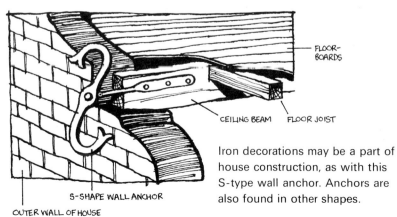

FLOOR-BOARDS

CEILING BEAM   FLOOR JOIST

S-SHAPE WALL ANCHOR

OUTER WALL OF HOUSE

Iron decorations may be a part of house construction, as with this S-type wall anchor. Anchors are also found in other shapes.

INSIDE HOUSES

An aumbry, or wall-cupboard.

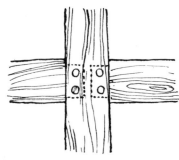

Wooden pegs, rather than metal, were used to join wooden beams.

A crown post support to the roof timbers.

Sometimes a date or a crest may be found on a fireback. Firedogs, for keeping wood fires in place, are worth investigating. This mediaeval fireplace has firedogs, and a baking oven along one side.

Carpenters used their own marks for identification.

This cast-iron decorated fireback dates from 1645.

Carpenters' numerals were marked on beams at the workshop, which made them easier to put together at the site.

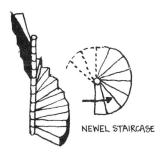

NEWEL STAIRCASE

A newel staircase can be inconvenient because of the different tread widths.

DOG LEG STAIRCASE

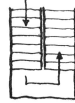

A dog leg staircase makes a sharp turn at a landing.

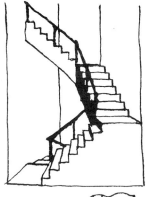

WELL STAIRCASE

A well staircase is formed leaving a hollow middle or 'well'.

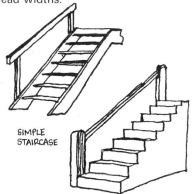

SIMPLE STAIRCASE

A simple staircase is really a ladder with the treads filled.

ELIZABETHAN COT

EARLY STUART TABLE/CHAIR

FARMHOUSE FOUR-POSTER BED

17TH CENTURY FOLDING OAK CHAIR

18TH CENTURY COCK-FIGHTING CHAIR

18TH CENTURY WHEELBACK CHAIR

18TH CENTURY SHIELD-BACK CHAIR BY HEPPLEWHITE

Antique furniture can give further clues to the date of a house.

SPECIAL HOUSES

Some old houses are open to the public. They can provide fascinating information about the family that once lived there. Furniture, utensils, even old toys and clothing help to create an image of the past. Quebec House, pictured above, in Westerham, Kent, is where General Wolfe grew up.

Kipling House in Villiers Street, London, has a round plaque on the wall recording when Rudyard Kipling the writer lived there. Many other London houses have similar blue plaques.

John 'Butcher' Morley built his house in 1710–14 in Halstead, Essex. Called Blue Bridge House, it bears the owner's arms over the door, showing that some tradesmen were able to rise in social class.

RURAL COMMUNITIES

If it is accurate to observe that the last 150 years have shown a marked drift towards urban living, it is probably equally true to note that in recent years this trend has not only been halted but reversed. Under the stress of modern life our cities have begun to decay. Urban renewal—a phrase as common to Asia and the Americas as to Europe—has become a political necessity. Our response to this call for urban renewal has been somewhat unexpected. Cities have been marginally improved, but our renewal has also included a perceptible shift from the towns. We have re-established links with the countryside almost as though we believe that a return to a more rural past will fortify us against contemporary pressures and problems.

However, the countryside has to be reached and in our efforts to open up the countryside for all we have already gone some way to destroying the very things we were hoping to rediscover. Parts of the Pennine Walk, for example, had to be closed during the summer of 1976 because the number of walkers using it was so great that the footpath was crumbling away. Keepers of the National Parks have repeatedly asked for legislation to be introduced to prevent cars (and their occupants) causing irreparable damage to areas of great natural beauty.

This desire for a greater appreciation of rural things can only be for the good. Providing that the countryside code is respected, farmers seem more than ever prepared to talk to young people about the nature of their work—the problems of animal husbandry, the types of crops, agricultural machinery, drainage. This interest can be extended by spending a day at the County Show (most counties hold one annually) and further deepened by visiting a museum of country life.

These museums have been introduced recently. Costumes, photographs, country crafts, old tools, traction engines and quaint equipment somehow continue to suggest that farming before it became dominated by the tractor was a more romantic activity than it is today—a viewpoint which should not be expressed too enthusiastically in the village pub!

Some folk museums are 'living'—certain days are set aside each week to show local craftsmen and women using traditional methods to make lace, to weave and spin, to make butter and to milk cows by hand. A visit to such a museum is also a useful way of discovering where local crafts may still be learned.

Often the demonstrators themselves run courses—perhaps at a nearby Evening Institute, a Village College, or through a branch of the Women's Institutes.

Not all rural crafts, however, are domestic. A village might still boast a smith, a thatcher, a stone mason or a reed weaver. If there is time, study the tools which are being used for these crafts. The adze was developed in the Middle East centuries before the birth of Christ. It's encouraging to discover that rural craftsmen are still using it to fashion wood today.

The village itself is also likely to reflect the past and present preoccupations of its parishioners. Memorials in the church might record a skirmish in the Civil War, a local catastrophe (as at Eyam in Derbyshire when the plague wiped out the majority of the population), or the life and death of a quixotic local dignitary. If a preaching cross and a pillory remind us of times that were, the lack of a bus service and 'for sale' notices above the village school may prompt the thought that village life can be harsh as well as quaint.

Before leaving a village, visit the shops, where a large range of goods may be packed incongruously into a small space. Spare a glance for the woodwork and the fittings, which somehow take us back to an age when milk was served from a churn, when all eggs were free range, and potatoes 7lb for 6p.

Villages

A village is a small community. It might have grown up around an industry. At Llanhilleth, in Gwent, rows of terraced houses were built for the coal miners.

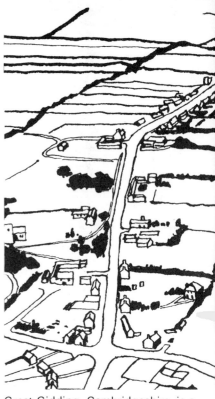

Great Gidding, Cambridgeshire, is a countryside village. Each house along the main street had its own smallholding behind it.

A Saxon village was compact. Northleach, Gloucestershire, on the River Leach is an example.

Litton, Derbyshire, is a Celtic-type straggling hill village.

Some villages are careful to build their houses in local materials so that they fit in with older buildings.

The special thing about this village, called Flash, is that it is the highest in England—462 metres above sea level. Flash means counterfeit money.

The village school in Aylburton, Gloucestershire, is an example of how different periods of architecture intermix. It incorporates Victorian and contemporary styles.

From this church in Morwenstow, Cornwall, Robert Hawker, the priest, preached against the wreckers— people who lured ships onto the rocks with lanterns and then looted the wrecks.

A village may have several churches with different architectural styles. Here, in Derbyshire, the Duffield Baptist Church has a number of interesting features.

The church in Eyam, Derbyshire. The village voluntarily isolated itself in 1665–66 when plague broke out to confine the disease.

A round tower from the time of Edward the Confessor dates this church in Haddiscoe, Norfolk. Round towers are said to indicate that water is nearby.

Gravestones can provide historical information about a village. The same families may still live there; possibly a shop or a business may bear the same name.

A barn can give many clues about the nature of farming in the area. This is a tithe barn in Cherhill, Wiltshire.

A church may have brasses on either the floor or walls. The brass at Stoke d'Abernon, Surrey, records the death of Anne Norbury and her children.

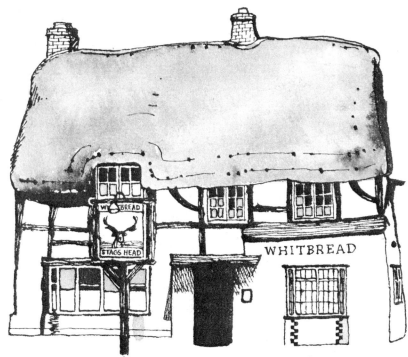

Public house signs are often a source of local information. They may indicate a local trade, family crest or something for which the village is famous. The Blue Bowl is in Polsham, Somerset.

A village pub often has a long history. The Stag's Head Inn, Wellesbourne, Warwickshire, is near a famous chestnut tree where, in 1872, Joseph Arch held a meeting that was the first step towards the formation of the National Agricultural Workers' Union.

The Brickmakers Arms, Barons Cross, Leominster (Hereford and Worcester).

The Howard Arms, Ilmington, Gloucestershire.

The Cheese Rollers, Shurdington, Gloucestershire, depicts a local annual custom.

Villages often contain relics from the past, such as the stocks in front of Eyam Hall, Derbyshire.

This round, twelfth century tower in Abernethy, Tayside, was once used as a refuge for the clergy in times of trouble.

An old village cross stands on the green at Monyash, Derbyshire.

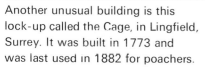

Another unusual building is this lock-up called the Cage, in Lingfield, Surrey. It was built in 1773 and was last used in 1882 for poachers.

A covered market cross would protect traders from the rain. This one, called the Butter Cross, is at Oakham, Leicestershire. It also contains the village stocks.

The Shambles at Shepton Mallet, Somerset, takes its name from the Saxon word 'scamel' which was the bench on which butchers cut their meat. The bench was very messy, hence the modern meaning.

Wymondham was granted the right to hold a market by King John in 1203, but this famous cross was not built until 1618. It has an outdoor stairway leading to the upper storey, and the pillars and beams are covered with the shapes of wood turning—tops, spindles and spoons—for which the town was once famous.

A butcher shop in Wymondham, Norfolk, advertises that it is a 'licensed dealer in game'.

This village shop in Brockweir, Gloucestershire, is also the local post office.

At a disused railway station in the Wye Valley the tracks have been filled in to form a picnic site.

Cottage gardens, such as this one with broad beans and beehives, are usually a part of the village scene.

A peaceful scene at the village pond at Tissington, Derbyshire.

A spring or pump was the village meeting place where people drew their water. This village pump is at Tillingham, Essex.

VILLAGE CUSTOMS

A village may have a local hunt.

Village fetes and carnivals which take place at different times of the year usually stem from old customs and beliefs. This is the carnival in Aylburton, Gloucestershire.

A traditional Herefordshire corn dolly.

In Abbots Bromley, Staffordshire, six horn dancers make a twenty-mile, twelve hour circuit of the parish on the first Monday after the 4th September.

Well decorating in Tissington, Derbyshire, is a thanksgiving, for tradition has it that the pure water saved many from the Black Death of 1348.

FOR HIS SHEEP THE SHEPHERD DIED

COUNTRY CRAFTS

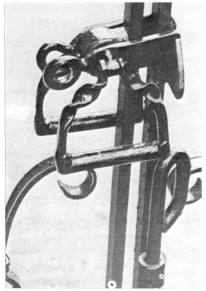

The blacksmith's forge was of vital importance to any village. It was here that people brought their horses to be shod or tools to be mended. Some still continue to operate—for the local community's horses, or for hand-casting ornamental iron.

The traditional craft of wrought ironwork is still carried on, but with more modern methods. Fixing ornamental parts is done with clips, nowadays aided by welding. The clips form an integral part of the design. The beauty and balance of a wrought iron gate adds a touch of decoration to a garden.

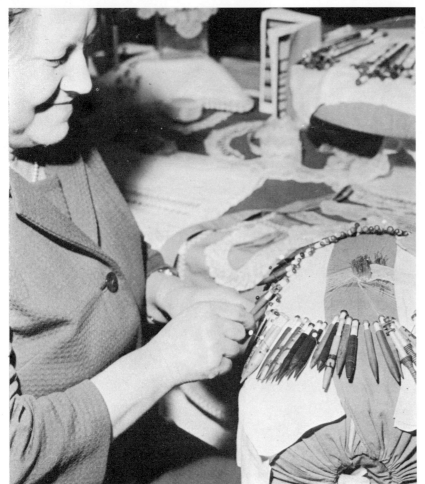

Lace making is a craft that is kept alive in some villages. In Totton, Hampshire, a lace maker adjusts lace bobbins.

In May some rivers will need to be 'weeded', which means cutting out some weeds and leaving others for fish to find food in.

Pottery has become very popular as a craft in recent years. It is often possible to visit a potter's workshop and watch things being made. Here, Barrie Naylor, a Gloucestershire potter, sits at his wheel.

Seven-straw plaiting is rather
difficult. The plait is held in the left
hand, the basket in front.

Sheep hurdles are now more
common in gardens than on farms.
This is how the shepherd used to
carry them. Hurdlemakers wove the
'wattles' with split hazel wands.

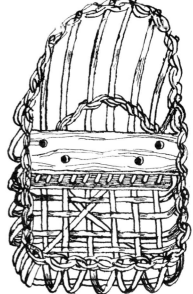

A coracle frame. Sometimes folk
museums will display products of
local craftsmen which serve as
illustrations of a past way of life.

Watercress growing has become a
much bigger business these days.
A watercress farm may have acres
of beds, and can harvest crops
throughout the year.

Water meadow farming has a four hundred year old tradition. It is a way of growing grass by flooding from the rivers. The water is diverted from the river by a weir and, by a network of trenches, it spreads over the meadow. Water from a chalk stream is best because it is usually warm and also provides minerals for the grass. Furrows in the meadow lead the water back to the main stream.

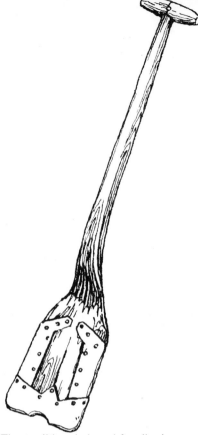

The traditional shovel for digging drains and drainage ditches.

In parts of the north and west of England fields have stone walls rather than hedges or fences. Dry-stone walls are made without the use of any mortar. In the two pictures above the stones are different. Those which have smooth corners were no doubt from an area near a river. On the right a dry-stone-waller practises his centuries-old craft.

The craft of making wagons and wooden wheels requires much skill. Here the iron tyre is fixed on the wooden wheel by the blacksmith. He slips the iron tyre over while hot, cools it with water, and as it contracts it binds the wheel tightly.

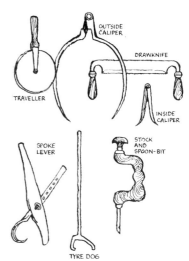

Each craft has its own traditional tools. These are the tools of a wheelwright.

An old farm wagon from Teigh, Leicestershire, traditionally painted bright ochre red.

How butter was made in the country, using a wooden churn.

CRAFT TOOLS

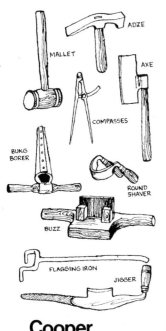

MALLET
ADZE
AXE
COMPASSES
BUNG BORER
ROUND SHAVER
BUZZ
FLAGGING IRON
JIGGER

Cooper

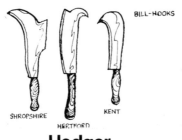

BILL-HOOKS
SHROPSHIRE
HERTFORD
KENT

Hedger

HOOKING KNIFE
STRAIGHT CHISEL
CURVED GOUGE
FISHTAIL

Woodcarver

BOWL-TURNING GOUGE

Wood turner

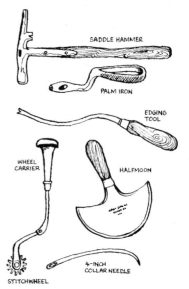

SADDLE HAMMER
PALM IRON
EDGING TOOL
WHEEL CARRIER
HALFMOON
STITCHWHEEL
4-INCH COLLAR NEEDLE

Saddle & harness maker

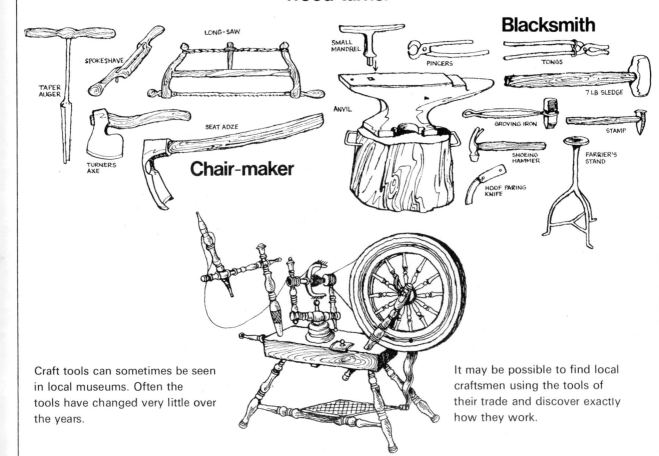

TAPER AUGER
SPOKESHAVE
LONG-SAW
SEAT ADZE
TURNERS AXE

Chair-maker

SMALL MANDREL
PINCERS
ANVIL
HOOF PARING KNIFE
SHOEING HAMMER
GROVING IRON
FARRIER'S STAND
STAMP
TONGS
7 LB SLEDGE

Blacksmith

Craft tools can sometimes be seen in local museums. Often the tools have changed very little over the years.

It may be possible to find local craftsmen using the tools of their trade and discover exactly how they work.

Farms

Rievaulx Abbey in Yorkshire was built by monks who came over from France in the twelfth century. The economy of the abbey depended upon sheep farming.

This enormous fourteenth century tithe barn in Alciston, Sussex, belonged to the grange of Battle Abbey.

This ruined pigeon house or dovecote once provided meat for the Monks' table at Battle Abbey.

A 700 year old wall painting from Cocking Church, Sussex, depicts a shepherd, with crook and dog.

A ruined defensive tower still stands at Welton Hall, a border farmhouse in Northumberland. Whenever there was any risk of attack, the animals would be rounded up into the tower for safety.

A stone sheep pen or pin fold was used to contain stray sheep. A wooden gate would have closed them in, until they were collected by their owners.

This old gabled barn in Waldron, Sussex, has double doors on the right where the old threshing floor used to be. Barns and farmhouses were usually built from local materials.

A Tudor granary was raised on straddle stones to prevent rats and mice from getting at the corn. Rodents could not climb over the mushroom shaped supports. This granary was preserved and rebuilt in the grounds of Cowdray Castle.

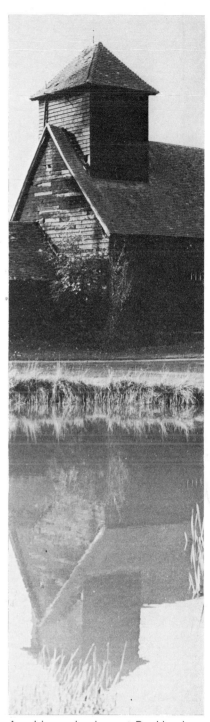

An old wooden barn at Buckland, Surrey. The architecture of barns and farm buildings makes a fascinating study. Materials and styles differ from one part of the country to another.

A wooden strapwork barn in Herefordshire shows one method of providing ventilation to the barn. The woven panels let in fresh air.

A brick barn in Herefordshire is ventilated by means of open-work brick which forms a decorative pattern on the end wall.

Some buildings on a farm serve a very specific purpose, as this one at Dumfries. It was built on to a barn to house a rotary thresher.

Dairy farm buildings usually include a silo tower or silage pit. Behind these silo towers are corrugated-iron farm buildings.

The concrete sides of this modern barn hold in the silage, while the upper part is usually used for storing straw.

This Herefordshire oast house is quite a different shape from the more familiar round oast houses found in Kent.

A Cumberland farmhouse and dry-stone wall are typical of the area.

Converted oast houses can make a lovely home, and still retain the original flavour of the builders.

A longhouse is the oldest type of farmhouse. It provided shelter for the farmer and his animals under one roof. This modernised Devon longhouse was extended to the left of the doorway in the 1860s.

This weatherboarded Essex farmhouse is typical of that part of the country.

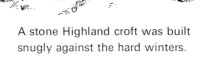

A stone Highland croft was built snugly against the hard winters.

FARM CROPS

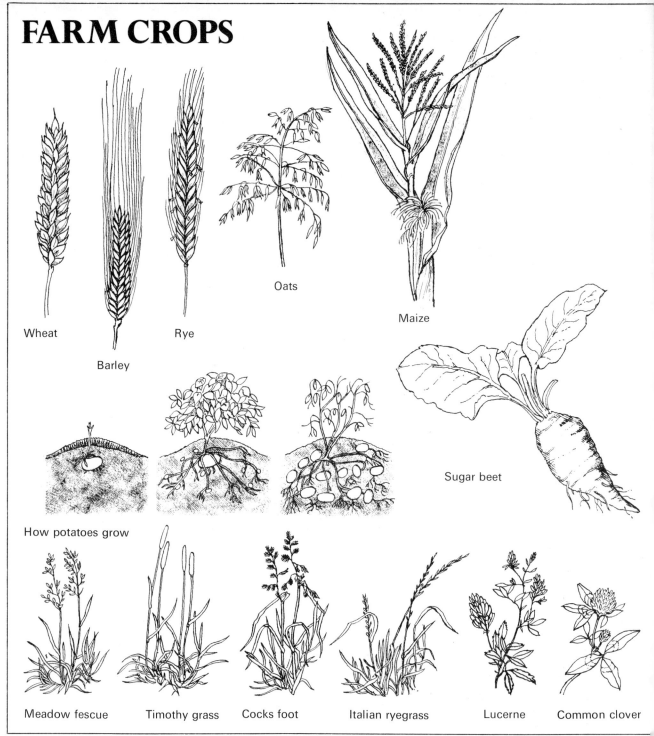

Wheat

Barley

Rye

Oats

Maize

Sugar beet

How potatoes grow

Meadow fescue

Timothy grass

Cocks foot

Italian ryegrass

Lucerne

Common clover

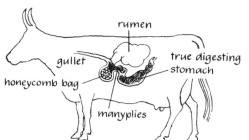

rumen

gullet

honeycomb bag

true digesting stomach

manyplies

Cattle are ruminants, feeding basically on grass. They have four stomachs, and each is used in turn until the grass is fully digested.

LIVESTOCK

A Friesian calf

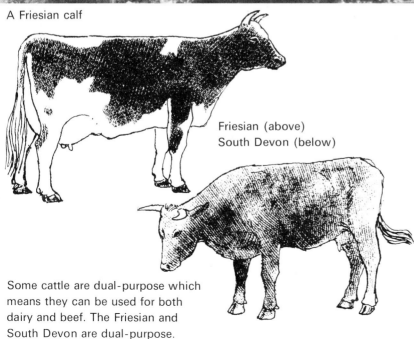

Friesian (above)
South Devon (below)

Some cattle are dual-purpose which means they can be used for both dairy and beef. The Friesian and South Devon are dual-purpose.

White Leghorn

Rhode Island Red

A cross between a Rhode Island Red and a White Leghorn produces a good egg-laying hybrid.

Turkey

101

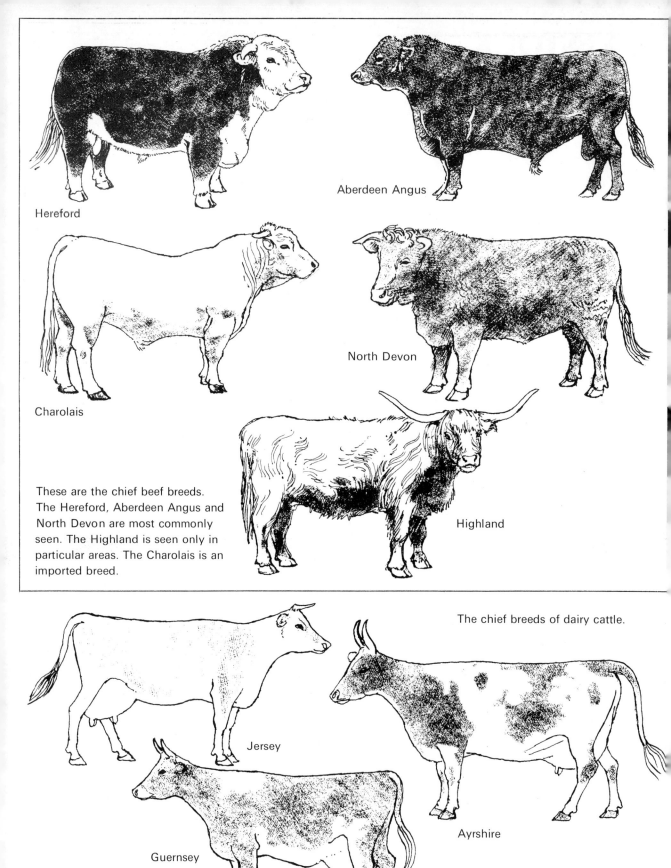

Hereford

Aberdeen Angus

Charolais

North Devon

These are the chief beef breeds.
The Hereford, Aberdeen Angus and
North Devon are most commonly
seen. The Highland is seen only in
particular areas. The Charolais is an
imported breed.

Highland

The chief breeds of dairy cattle.

Jersey

Guernsey

Ayrshire

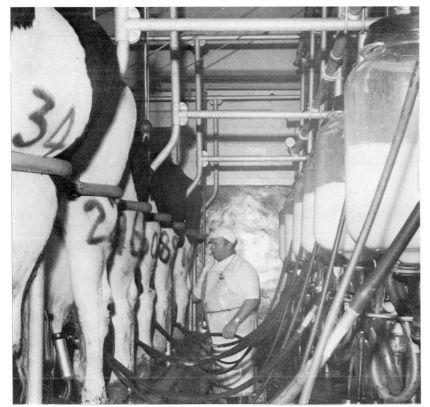

A hundred cows can now be milked in the time it took a milkmaid to do three or four. This is a herring bone milking parlour where the cows stand slantwise.

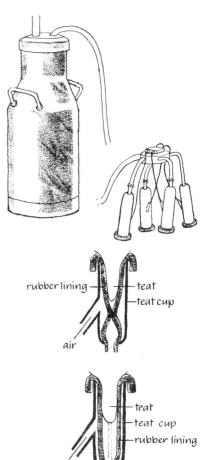

The milking machine imitates the sucking action of a calf. The four cups are lined with rubber and there is a space between the lining and the outer wall into which air is rhythmically pumped.

The milk tanker holds 2000 gallons and collects milk from farms.

Up to a quarter million pints a day are bottled at this dairy in Preston, Lancashire.

A full automated buttermaking unit at the Alfreton creamery.

Cheviot

Dartmoor

There are more than thirty different breeds of sheep. These, the hill sheep, can survive in hard conditions chiefly because their thick, oily wool protects them from the cold. Pure-bred flocks are found chiefly in hilly country.

Welsh Mountain

Blackface

Devon

Breeds of long-wool sheep

Leicester

Romney Marsh

Lincoln

Sheep dogs are invaluable to the farmer. Here a Border collie is on duty on a Northumberland hill farm. A good dog takes two or three years to be trained.

Hampshire Down

South Down

Suffolk

Dorset Horn

Breeds of short-wool sheep

In June or July all the sheep are sheared. A skilled shearer can clip as many as 200 sheep in one day. About a fortnight after shearing the sheep are dipped or sprayed against parasites.

Large White

Landrace

Pig farming is increasing in Britain. A great deal of research has gone into pig breeding, and a number of hybrids or cross-breeds have been tested for rate of growth. These three breeds are used for crossing.

Wessex Saddleback

105

FARM MACHINERY

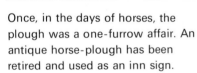

Once, in the days of horses, the plough was a one-furrow affair. An antique horse-plough has been retired and used as an inn sign.

Some farmers still prefer to plough with horses, but mainly the job is done with a tractor. A modern ploughman can manage seven furrows at once.

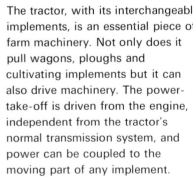

The tractor, with its interchangeable implements, is an essential piece of farm machinery. Not only does it pull wagons, ploughs and cultivating implements but it can also drive machinery. The power-take-off is driven from the engine, independent from the tractor's normal transmission system, and power can be coupled to the moving part of any implement.

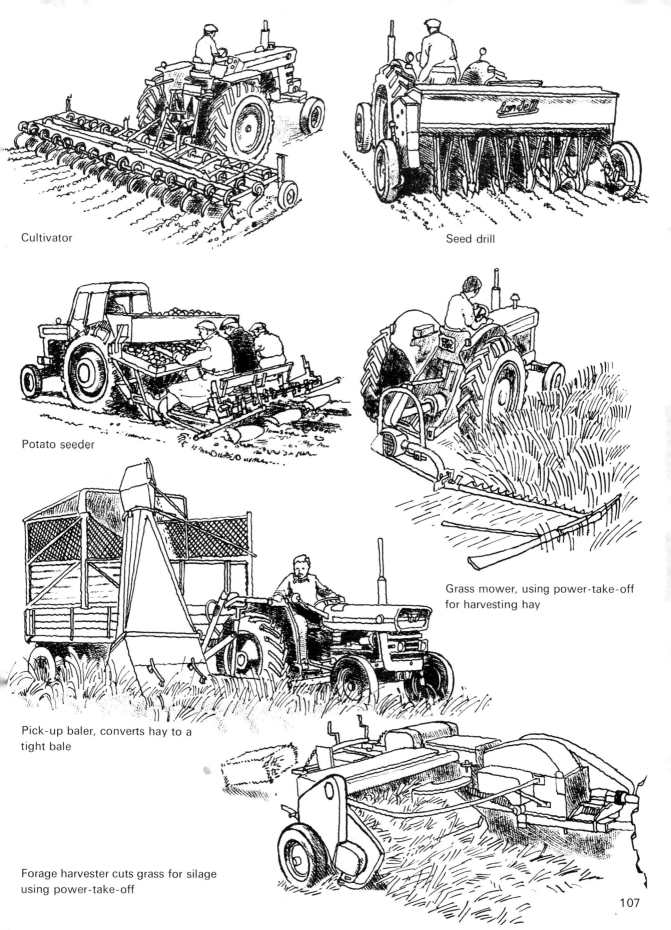

Cultivator

Seed drill

Potato seeder

Grass mower, using power-take-off for harvesting hay

Pick-up baler, converts hay to a tight bale

Forage harvester cuts grass for silage using power-take-off

107

A combine harvester cuts off corn stalks close to the ground. The stalks are carried to a threshing drum, inside which are beaters. Most of the grain falls through the grating. The straw and chaff are thown out onto the field.

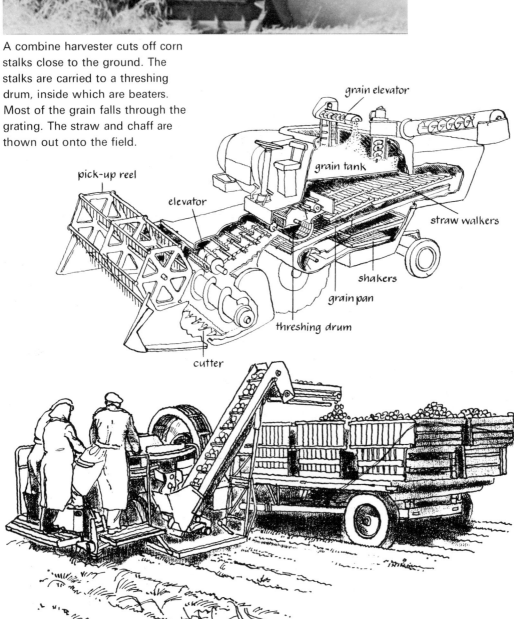

grain elevator

grain tank

pick-up reel

elevator

straw walkers

shakers

grain pan

threshing drum

cutter

Potato harvesters vary from quite simple ones to those which lift and clean the potatoes, remove stalks, and drop them onto a sorting platform.

CHURCHES & MONASTERIES

During the reign of Pope Gregory the Great, Augustine led a party of Benedictine monks to Britain to convert the Angles. He was well received by Bertha, the Christian wife of Ethelbert of Kent, and the King and his court were baptized. So it was that Christianity returned to Britain, and Canterbury, rather than London or Winchester, became its religious capital. Perhaps 'returned' seems an odd word to choose, but it would be incorrect to think that Augustine's mission of 597 marked the beginning of Christian belief on these islands.

There are, of course, legends which link Britain with the Christians of the early church. Some say that St Peter and St Paul preached here, others that Joseph of Arimathea hid the Holy Grail near Glastonbury. But there are facts too. Alban, a prominent Roman citizen of Verulamium was executed in 304 for befriending a priest, an event which was to make him the first of a long line of Britain's saints and martyrs. The Celtic church, a much more loosely knit organisation, continued to preach the Gospels to the people of Scotland, Ireland and Wales long after the last legionary had returned to defend Rome. St Patrick and St David owed no obedience to the Pope.

Augustine's mission, however, marked a new beginning, an expansion of the Roman church. In 633 at Whitby Abbey, the Celtic and Roman churches agreed to unite. The differences, over such doctrinal matters as the date of Easter, were settled. The whole of Britain could be brought under one faith. The history of the church from 633 onwards is an eventful one. The country was divided into seven kingdoms, not all of which were Christian. Such domestic harmony as existed was soon to be shattered. The heathen Northmen appeared. They first ravaged the country and then settled in it. It was not until the Danes themselves became Christian in 878 that Gregory's dream of a Christian Britain was finally realised.

Church and State were closely knit. A king was converted, and so were his people; a Danish army was defeated, and baptism was written into the peace treaty. This association has continued to the present day. Our churches record in stone, wood and glass both religious and political events.

The martyrdom of Thomas à Becket, for example, was a reflection of the tensions caused by such a union. The manner of his death was probably more valuable in economic terms to Canterbury than any contribution he could have made during his lifetime. The pilgrims who subsequently knelt at his shrine became part of the life style of the mediaeval age. In more recent times, the destruction of Coventry led to the creation of a new cathedral. It stands next to the ruins of the old, to proclaim reconciliation.

The church from Saxon times to the present day has never avoided the political, economic and social tensions of its age. But it has always managed to represent continuity—a continuity we are able to appreciate as we wander round abbey church, cathedral, or tiny chapel. But in the very richness of our heritage lie dangers. It is so easy to be swept away by the grandeur of Lincoln, Exeter, York, Ely or Gloucester that in the process we overlook the beauty of less well-known buildings, buildings which may have a saxon tower, Norman chancel, Gothic nave, hammer beam roof or Wren spire. It's a pity if we allow the great cathedrals to eclipse the parish churches, which contain much to interest the social historian, the ecclesiastic and the artist. Brasses, quaint tombs, primitive fire fighting equipment, chained libraries, chapels that once housed the village school, documents recording plague and revolution, carving and wall paintings—our churches are a wonderful source for discovering our heritage.

Many of the great churches which once belonged to the religious orders—Benedictine, Carthusian, Cistercian, Premonstratensian, Trinitarian—are now little more than attractive ruins, destroyed by wind and rain, as much as by Henry VIII's commissioners. Yet it requires no great leap of imagination to see in our mind's eye these buildings as they once were, and wonder at how so great a structure could be built with so few mechanical aids.

The churches of Britain reflect our history. Their architectural styles span the years from Saxon to the present day. And so do the people they commemorate—Arden and Alfred, Botolph and Chad, Felix and Giles, Oswald and Osyth, Swithin and Wilfred. History is people. Perhaps it is because our churches reflect the life of people from birth to death that they hold for us, even in these secular days, unending fascination.

THE DEVELOPMENT OF CHURCHES

The first churches were probably built of wood, though some stone churches, like this one at Bradford-on-Avon, Wiltshire, were built in Saxon times.

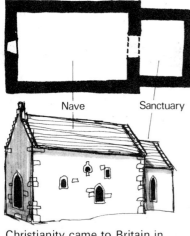

Nave   Sanctuary

Christianity came to Britain in Roman times. The earliest churches consisted of a nave (where the congregation worshipped) and the sanctuary which contained the altar. Occasionally the sanctuary was rounded at the east end.

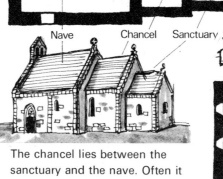

Nave   Chancel   Sanctuary

The chancel lies between the sanctuary and the nave. Often it contains the choir stalls and is on a slightly higher level than the nave.

Aisles were added by widening the nave. They were useful for processions as well as providing extra accommodation. The north aisle is usually older than the south aisle because the south side of the church was used for burial.

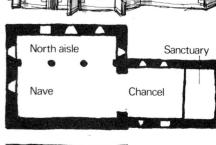

North aisle   Sanctuary

Nave   Chancel

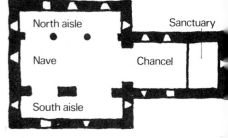

North aisle   Sanctuary

Nave   Chancel

South aisle

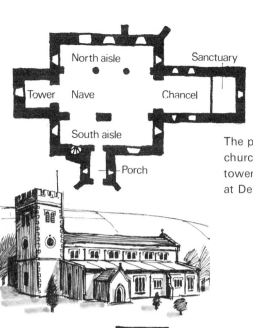

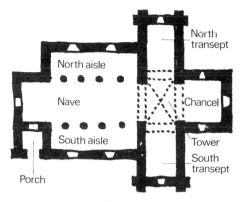

The porch is the entrance to the church. In the plan on the left the tower is placed at the west end, as at Dent Church, Yorkshire.

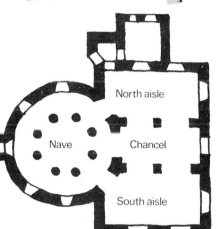

The Holy Sepulchre Church in Cambridge has a circular Norman nave. Although the shape of the church may alter the terms remain the same.

Churches with transepts often have aisles as well. The difference between chancel and sanctuary is sometimes not shown on the plans. The sanctuary is the small, enclosed space where the altar stands within the chancel.

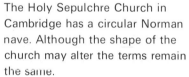

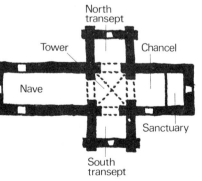

Some churches have their towers between the sanctuary and the nave. On either side of the tower lie the transepts. They make the plan of the church look like a cross.

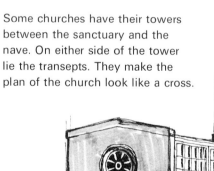

Modern churches sometimes follow the traditional plan. However, new building materials have led to new designs, as this one in Harlow New Town, Essex.

PARTS OF A CHURCH

This cutaway view of a traditionally planned church shows a cross-shaped plan, with transepts and aisles.

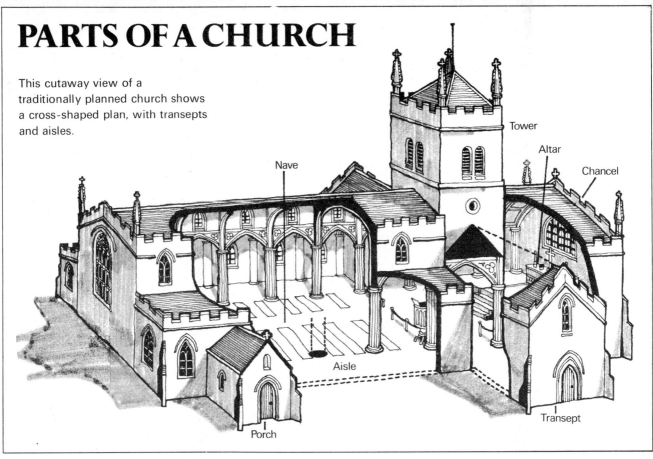

Tower

Altar

Chancel

Nave

Aisle

Transept

Porch

OUTSIDE CHURCHES

The yew tree was sacred in pagan Britain. It was customary in Mediterranean countries to plant them in graveyards and Roman priests may have brought the custom to Britain.

A lych-gate was used to shelter a body as it was moved from a cart to the parish bier that was wheeled to the church. Lych is the Saxon word for dead body. This is a 17th century gate at Worth, Sussex.

A church graveyard may have many interesting tombs, or a cross or memorial. A realistic skull is carved into this eighteenth century family tomb.

A churchyard cross, such as this mediaeval cross at Castle Rising, Norfolk, was often used for preaching and for making proclamations.

The most common shape for a weather vane is the cockerel, the emblem of St Peter. This old weathervane has been replaced, and given a home inside Church Handborough Church, Oxfordshire.

Barfreystone in Kent has no belfry, so the bell is hung in a yew tree.

Special crosses, called consecration crosses, were carved or painted on the side of the church after it had been dedicated by the bishop.

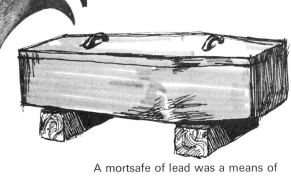

A mortsafe of lead was a means of preventing body snatchers stealing the dead before burial. It dates from the late 18th century.

The tower was sometimes a place of refuge. This eleventh century round tower at Blessingham, Norfolk, is made from flint.

This four-storied Saxon tower at Bishopstone, Sussex, had a corbel-table and cap added later by the Normans.

The Norman tower of Old Shoreham, Sussex.

A saddleback tower usually has one gable, but Fingest, in Buckinghamshire, has two.

A transitional tower at new Shoreham shows the change from round to pointed-arch windows.

Occasionally octagonal towers were built, as this one at Marsh Baldon, Oxfordshire.

A broach spire has a triangular chamfer at each corner, as this fouteenth century one has at Detling, Kent. The spire is really an extension to the tower.

A parapet spire, Cassington, Oxfordshire, All spires are post-Norman.

This church in Rye, Sussex, has gilded clock jacks that strike the hour. The purpose of a tower and its spire was to house the bells, though some towers also made excellent landmarks for sailors.

Perpendicular towers like Charing, Kent, often have an outside stair turret to the belfry and roof.

A thirteenth century tower at Long Sutton, Lincolnshire, has a lead spire and four pinnacles. Lead weathers white, copper turns green.

Louth, in Lincolnshire, has a parapet spire with flying buttresses. The stone knobs, called crockets, help steeplejacks.

St Mary-le-Bow, Cheapside, London (left) has a spire which is really a steeple, built by Sir Christopher Wren in 1680. St Clement Danes (right) is also a Wren church whose bells ring out 'oranges and lemons'. There is still a special service during which children are presented with oranges and lemons.

Many old clock mechanisms have been preserved by churches, some are still in good working order.

Gargoyles are water spouts taking rain water off the roof. Often they are carved into demons to frighten away evil spirits, as these on Garsington Church, Oxfordshire.

Doorways can make an interesting study when looking at churches. Many churches are built in limestone, which is found right across Britain. In some areas granite, flint, red sandstone or brick and even wood are used. Stone carving may stand up well if the stone is hard and has not weathered. This beautifully decorated, early Norman doorway is the south entrance to Barfreystone Church, Kent.

Mason's marks were cut lightly into the dressed stone to identify a particular stone-mason's work.

A Saxon sundial was carved over the door of March Baldon, Oxfordshire.

Scratch dials, with a hole for a rod to cast a shadow.

117

INSIDE CHURCHES

A Saxon chancel arch at Escomb, County Durham.

Both arches and windows give clues to the date of a church. Sometimes different styles are found within the same church. These are Norman arches at Melbourne, Derbyshire.

These transitional arches are found at New Shoreham, Sussex.

Perpendicular arches can be seen at Chipping Campden, Gloucestershire.

Early English arches at Stone, Kent.

WINDOWS

Saxon

Norman

Transitional

Exterior views

Interior views

A low-side window (Melton Constable, Norfolk)

Early English

Decorated

Perpendicular

Tudor

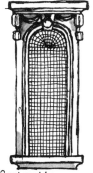

Restoration Stuart

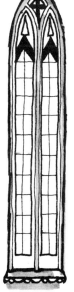

Early Twentieth Century

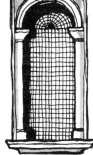

Early Georgian

Late Georgian

Regency

Victorian Gothic

Late Victorian

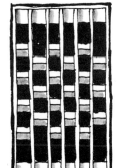

Contemporary

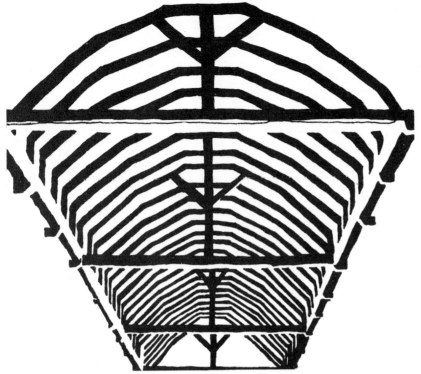

The roof of a church may be built on stone, wood, or wood and plaster. Decorations, paintings, and carvings all make an interesting study. Some roofs look like the inside of a ship turned upside down. The word nave obviously has a nautical derivation. This is a king-post roof, Lyminster, Sussex.

St John's Chapel, Ewelme, Oxfordshire has a splendidly carved roof.

Because this church in Plaxtol, Kent, was built during the Reformation it is not dedicated to any saint. It has a seventeenth century hammer beam roof.

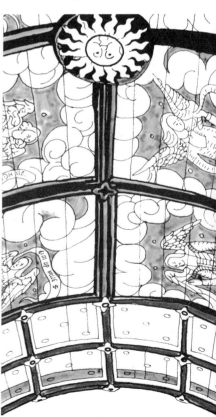

A brightly painted wagon roof.

Careful examination of the beams in Charing Church, Kent, show that they are painted to look like carving. It is a tie beam roof, dated 1592, and inscribed 'ER 34'.

Quadripartite, thirteenth century stone vaulted roof at New Shoreham, Sussex.

Vaulted roofs provided great scope for decoration. This is lierne vaulting, fourteenth century, from Tewkesbury choir, Gloucestershire.

Fourteenth century tierceron vaulting.

This fan vaulting at North Leigh in Oxfordshire dates from the fifteenth century. The fan shapes create a lovely sweeping pattern.

A carved roof boss from the south porch of Stoke-by-Nayland Church, Suffolk.

A carved stone corbel looks out in Ewelme Church, Oxfordshire. Corbels support roof timbers or vaulting.

Look for curiously sculpted Norman capitals such as these at Old Shoreham, Sussex.

Carved stone musicians play bagpipes and twin pipes.

DECORATION

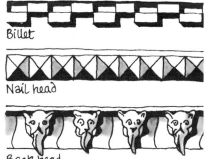

Billet

Nail head

Beak head

Chevron or Zigzag

Double cone

Cable

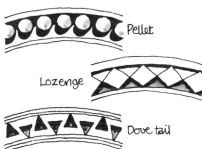

Pellet

Lozenge

Dove tail

Norman decoration

Dog tooth

Three-leaf flower

Early English

Ball flower

Tablet flower

Decorated

Perpendicular

Brattishing

Tudor rose

Tudor

Stories of saints, kings, poets, explorers and artists were all recorded in stained glass. Above is a merchant ship from 1530. Below, a fifteenth century angel playing a rebeck.

Decoration around windows and arches is another reliable method of dating a building, particularly if the motifs are studied together with the shape of windows, doorways, columns and arches and with roof styles.

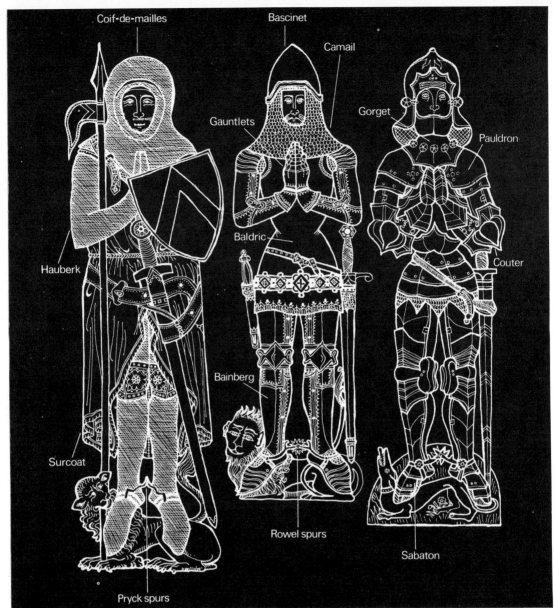

Coif-de-mailles

Bascinet

Camail

Gorget

Pauldron

Gauntlets

Baldric

Haubert

Couter

Bainberg

Surcoat

Rowel spurs

Sabaton

Pryck spurs

Changing styles in armour are shown by these church brasses. From left to right: Sir John D'Abernon, Sheriff of Surrey, 1277, the oldest known brass in England (Stoke D'Abernon Church, Surrey); a member of the Dalison family, about 1400, (Laughton, Lincolnshire); Edmond Clere, 1488, (Stokesby, Norfolk).

The tomb of Ralph and Katheren Green in Lowick, Northamptonshire, shows them carved in alabaster, holding hands.

Cresset stones were an early form of lighting. The holes were filled with oil and lighted wicks were floated in it. They are rare.

A rood screen made of wood or stone sometimes separates the nave from the chancel. This fifteenth century screen in Scarning Church, Norfolk, is carved from wood. Many were pulled down at the Reformation.

A sedilia is a seat. This triple sedilia is at Cobham Church, Kent. Next to it is a piscina, a shallow basin used for washing sacred vessels after Mass. These are usually found on the south wall, near the altar.

Pulpits came to be an essential part of church furniture. This Jacobean wood pulpit is in Beckley Church, Oxfordshire. It has a sounding board above.

A fourteenth century wooden lectern, from which the Bible is read, Detling, Kent.

A typical West Country square-headed bench end in Braunton Church, Devon.

A reredos is the carved screen behind the altar. This plaster one from about 1400 is at Thaxted, Essex.

Chests were used to keep registers, vestments, and plate. This Saxon dugout chest is from Wimborne Minster, Dorset.

Choir seats which fold up, called misericords, often have charming carvings underneath. At Etchingham, Kent, a fourteenth century misericord tells a story.

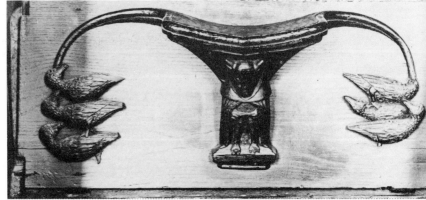

A Norman font with simple cable decoration, at St Enedoc in Cornwall.

The font, containing water for baptisms, could be made of several materials. This lead font at Brookland, Kent, dates from the twelfth century. It shows all the twelve signs of the zodiac and the farming activity for each month.

A twelfth century font in St Nicholas's Church, Brighton, Sussex, depicts the last supper.

At Ewelme, Oxfordshire, the font is covered by an elaborately carved wooden canopy. It was intended to protect the holy water from being stolen by witches. The canopy can be raised by a pulley.

Monasteries

By the end of the sixth century the Benedictines, called the 'Black Monks' because of their robes, were strongly established in Italy. St Augustine was chosen to bring Christianity to Britain, and in 597 he and his monks landed in Kent. He established his monastery at Canterbury which became a cathedral as well.

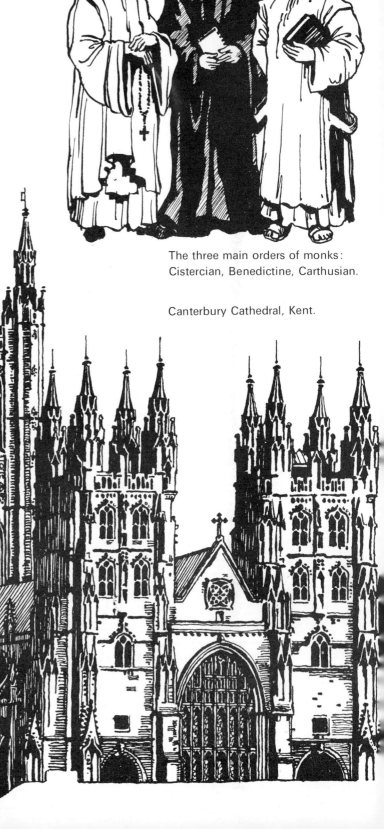

The three main orders of monks: Cistercian, Benedictine, Carthusian.

Canterbury Cathedral, Kent.

Part of Malmesbury Abbey Church is now used as the parish church.

Women as well as men lived in religious communities. There were some 'shared' monasteries. Here are grass-covered remains of Watton Priory, Humberside—a 'double' house of monks and nuns.

The builders of St Botolph's Priory, Colchester, Essex, used many Roman bricks from local Roman ruins.

A thirteenth century dovecote remains at Penman Priory, Anglesey, Gwynedd.

WHERE THE MONKS LIVED

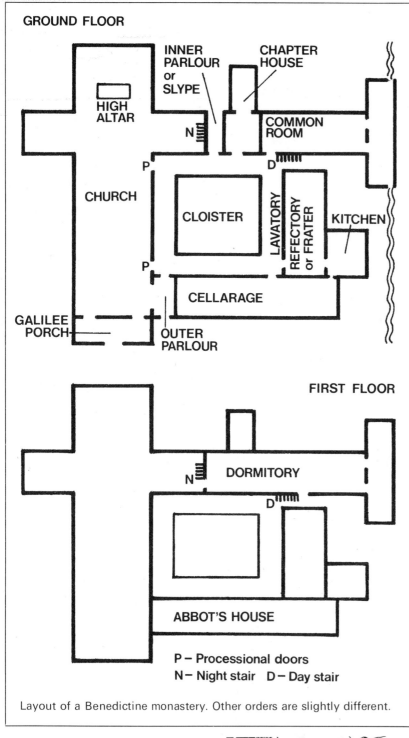

GROUND FLOOR

HIGH ALTAR

CHURCH

INNER PARLOUR or SLYPE

CHAPTER HOUSE

N

COMMON ROOM

P

P

CLOISTER

LAVATORY

REFECTORY or FRATER

KITCHEN

D

CELLARAGE

GALILEE PORCH

OUTER PARLOUR

FIRST FLOOR

N

DORMITORY

D

ABBOT'S HOUSE

P – Processional doors
N – Night stair   D – Day stair

Layout of a Benedictine monastery. Other orders are slightly different.

Food for the Abbot's guests, often very important ones, was prepared in his kitchen. This one is at Glastonbury Abbey.

Before dining, the monks washed at the lavatorium. This was a low stone trough, often with a highly decorated cover. Kirkham Priory, North Yorkshire.

All that is left of a lavatorium drain at Cambuskenneth Abbey, Stirling, Scotland, is bare stones.

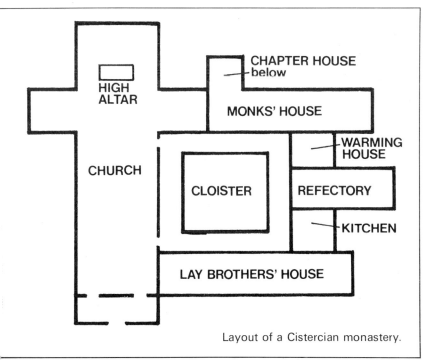

Layout of a Cistercian monastery.

The cloister was a covered way that led from the church to buildings around it. These cloister seats are from Byland Abbey, North Yorkshire.

A recess in the wall of Fountains Abbey, North Yorkshire, held a wax tablet stating monks' daily duties.

Once the abbey gatehouse (above left) now the entrance to a farm. The cloister well at Fountains Abbey, and the finely carved west front of the chapter house (below left).

131

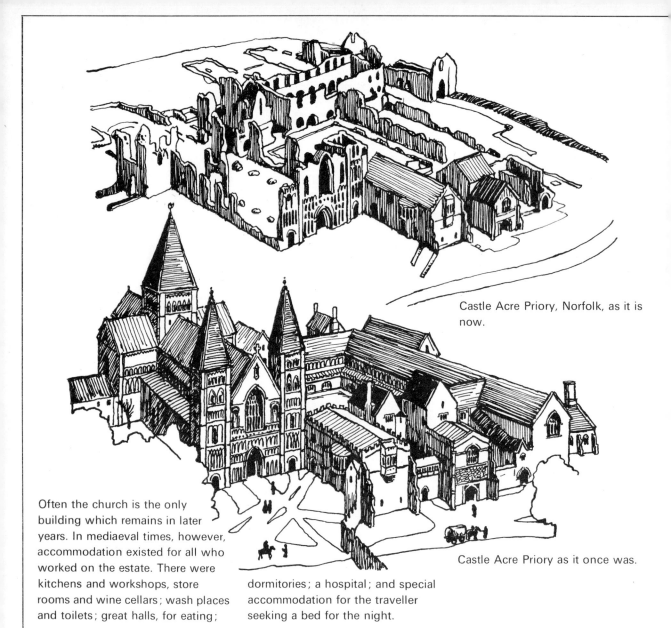

Castle Acre Priory, Norfolk, as it is now.

Castle Acre Priory as it once was.

Often the church is the only building which remains in later years. In mediaeval times, however, accommodation existed for all who worked on the estate. There were kitchens and workshops, store rooms and wine cellars; wash places and toilets; great halls, for eating; dormitories; a hospital; and special accommodation for the traveller seeking a bed for the night.

The fourth side of the cloister in a Benedictine monastery was used for storage. Cellars were built on the ground floor, joining an outer parlour. Through this goods were taken to be sold, such as wool and cloth, and provisions were brought in. The lay brothers' refectory at Fountains Abbey, North Yorkshire, became a cellar when the Black Death reduced the staff of the abbey.

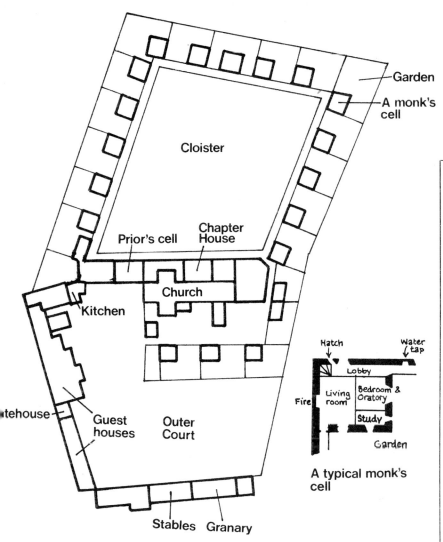

Cloister

Garden

A monk's cell

Prior's cell

Chapter House

Church

Kitchen

Guest houses

Outer Court

…tehouse

Stables   Granary

Layout of a Carthusian monastery—Mount Grace Priory, North Yorkshire.

The monk's cell (below) shows a food hatch next to the door.

Hatch

Water tap

Lobby

Fire

Living room

Bedroom & Oratory

Study

Garden

A typical monk's cell

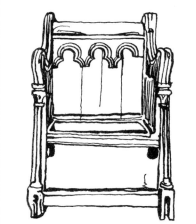

Prior's wooden seat in Little Dunmow Priory, Essex.

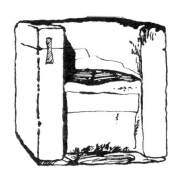

Stone sanctuary chair from Beverly Minister, Humberside.

St Augustine's chair of stone, Canterbury.

133

The refectory, or frater, was on the third side of the cloister. This pulpit is in the refectory of Beaulieu Abbey, Hampshire, which is now used as a church.

This Cistercian pottery from York dates from the early sixteenth century. It is decorated with a stag's head. Pottery was usually made by the monks themselves.

The monks' dormitory, or dorter, was a long, bare apartment. In the later Middle Ages it might have been partitioned. A night stair would lead directly from the dormitory to the church. The dorter range of Cleeve Abbey, Somerset, is pictured from the cloister.

THE MONASTIC CHURCH

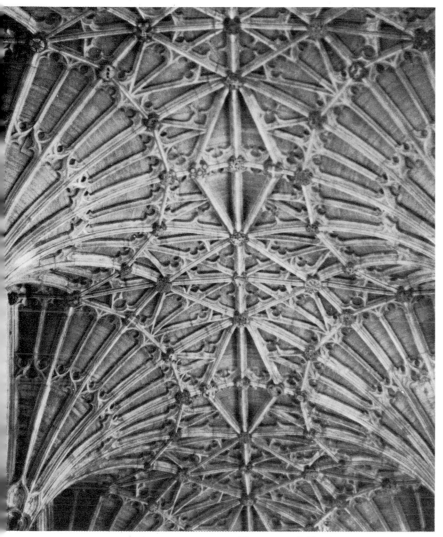

The choir of Jedburgh Abbey, Roxburghshire in Scotland is in Romanesque style.

The nave of Sherborne Abbey in Dorset was built with beautiful fan vaulting.

This richly carved prior's door, c. 1170, is at Ely Cathedral, Cambridgeshire.

At Wells Cathedral, Somerset, a late fourteenth century astronomical clock is attributed to Peter Lightfoot, a Benedictine monk.

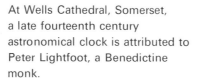

Craftsmanship in wood, stone and metal were features in the monastic church. This bronze sanctuary knocker is from Durham Cathedral, Durham.

Porch sculpture from Malmesbury Abbey, Wiltshire.

An aumbrey, which was a small safe for vessels, a piscina and a double sedilia in the quire of Tynemouth Priory, Tyne & Wear.

Stone coffins at St Andrew's Priory, Fifeshire, Scotland.

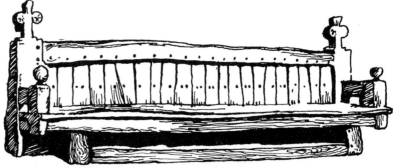

A bench for infirm monks in Winchester Cathedral, Hampshire.

136

CASTLES

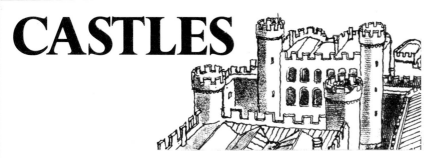

The mediaeval world saw the flowering of architecture in two distinct areas—ecclesiastical and military. Could we have visited 14th century Rochester, for example, we would have noticed that monastery and castle dominated the town. All other buildings were overshadowed —for in size, concept and flamboyance each fulfilled its purpose, to emphasise the power of God in Heaven and the strength of His rulers upon earth. Castles— strongholds held by a lord—do not predate the Norman period, although we somewhat lazily and incorrectly use the term to describe fortified hill town, Roman fort and Saxon camp.

The first castle built in Britain dates from the reign of Edward the Confessor. Richard, a Norman Knight, was given permission to fortify his house in Shropshire. Nothing much remains of it today— some overgrown stone-work, shrubby hillocks concealing defensive outworks, a steep tree-covered mound where once stood the keep. But the authorisation of his castle foreshadowed things to come.

William's victory at Hastings meant that Norman rather than Anglo-Saxon techniques of government, warfare and building would be practised in England. William did not intend simply to colonize England. He determined to settle here. To achieve this his followers needed to be secure, and defensive positions were therefore created. A circular mound of earth—a motte—was thrown up. Much of the earth for the mound was dug from around its base. Thus a ditch was formed which, when filled with water, became the moat. The mound was flattened on top and a wooden fence, or palisade, was built. Inside this a wooden house accommodated the Lord and his retainers. The castle was further extended with a bailey, which was a large courtyard beyond the motte. The bailey was also banked and palisaded, its ditch joining that which ran round the motte. This extension provided space for storage, stables, workshops and a chapel. It was also an outer defence for the Lord's stronghold.

It was from these primitive beginnings that the castle developed. The wooden strongholds were rebuilt in stone, the pattern of motte and bailey retained and natural defences, rivers and small hills, were built into the building whenever appropriate.

The new stone castles which replaced the hundred or so wooden castles of William's reign did not all follow an identical pattern. Most of the early keeps were rectangular, but shell keeps (as at Restormel, Cornwall) were not uncommon. To make the keep more secure, a surrounding wall, the curtain, broken only by a heavily defensive gatehouse was added.

But the great square keeps did not answer all the problems of warefare. The visibility of the defenders was limited and the corners of the keep were the weakest part of the whole structure. Indeed it was probably the development of the ram and the mine that caused the castle builders to modify their design. The mine was not an explosive. Sappers went forward and, protected by a wooden screen, dug a pit beneath the foundations of a wall, usually at a corner. The wall above the hole was propped with wooden struts. The hole was filled with dry timber and animal fat and fired. The fire burned the supporting struts and the wall, now unsupported, fell to the ground. The curved keeps were easier to defend.

Castles tended to develop outwards. The keep was protected by so many walls that its strategic importance declined, and finally it was done away with altogether. A great wall surrounded by a moat was considered sufficient defence.

During the reign of Edward I, however, castle design underwent a much more fundamental change. The keep was brought forward from the centre of the castle to the very front. To make these keep-gatehouse castles even less vulnerable one thing further was needed . . . to keep an enemy as far from the gatehouse as possible. The solution was to construct the inner walls and towers so that they overlooked the outer walls. But even as the military architects perfected their designs, a change was taking place in the nature of warfare . . . the development of gunpowder.

Castles went on being built in brick as well as stone, but their importance declined. A hundred years were to pass, however, before gunpowder finally came into its own. The great civil war marked the end of stationary warfare around fixed defensive strongholds.

THE DEVELOPMENT OF CASTLES

The very first castles were little more than wooden forts, consisting of a motte, the circular mound of earth; a palisade, the wooden fence; and a wooden tower.

A drawing from the Bayeux Tapestry shows workmen building the motte of Hastings Castle.

The castle was often extended by adding a bailey. This was a courtyard beyond the motte. It was also banked and palisaded.

The remains of Pickering Castle, Yorkshire, show the motte and walls.

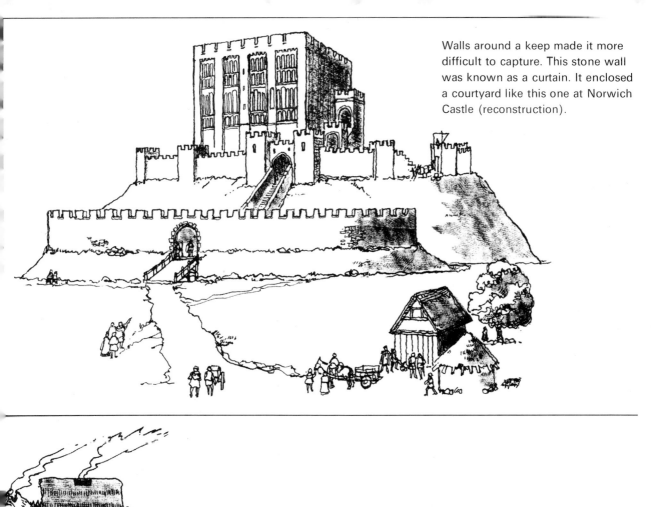

Walls around a keep made it more difficult to capture. This stone wall was known as a curtain. It enclosed a courtyard like this one at Norwich Castle (reconstruction).

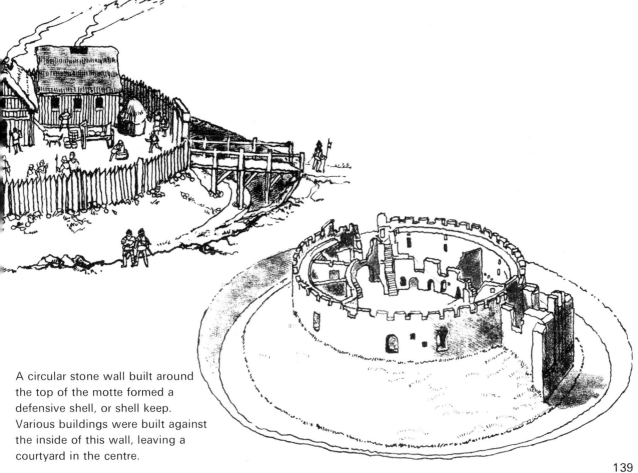

A circular stone wall built around the top of the motte formed a defensive shell, or shell keep. Various buildings were built against the inside of this wall, leaving a courtyard in the centre.

Rochester Castle.

N. E Stair

Well

Bridge pit

Step up

Site of Turret

Most early keeps were square, like this Norman keep at Goodrich Castle, Herefordshire.

The great square keeps did not answer all the problems of warfare. Corners were weak and could be mined or battered. This square Norman keep at Rochester Castle is about thirty metres high. The plan is of the ground floor.

Chamber

Drain and sink

Garderobe

Lower Hall

Kitchen

Main Entrance

Vestibule

At Orford Castle, Suffolk, the keep was built on a polygonal plan. Each turret supported its neighbour and the ground below could be seen from above. Towers were erected along the curtain walls for greater protection.

141

Mural towers along the curtain wall of White Castle, Gwent, were built with a curved front for strength.

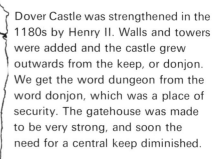

Dover Castle was strengthened in the 1180s by Henry II. Walls and towers were added and the castle grew outwards from the keep, or donjon. We get the word dungeon from the word donjon, which was a place of security. The gatehouse was made to be very strong, and soon the need for a central keep diminished.

Conway Castle in Gwynedd has well preserved battlements, with mural towers and bartizans, small turrets which jut out from the wall of a tower.

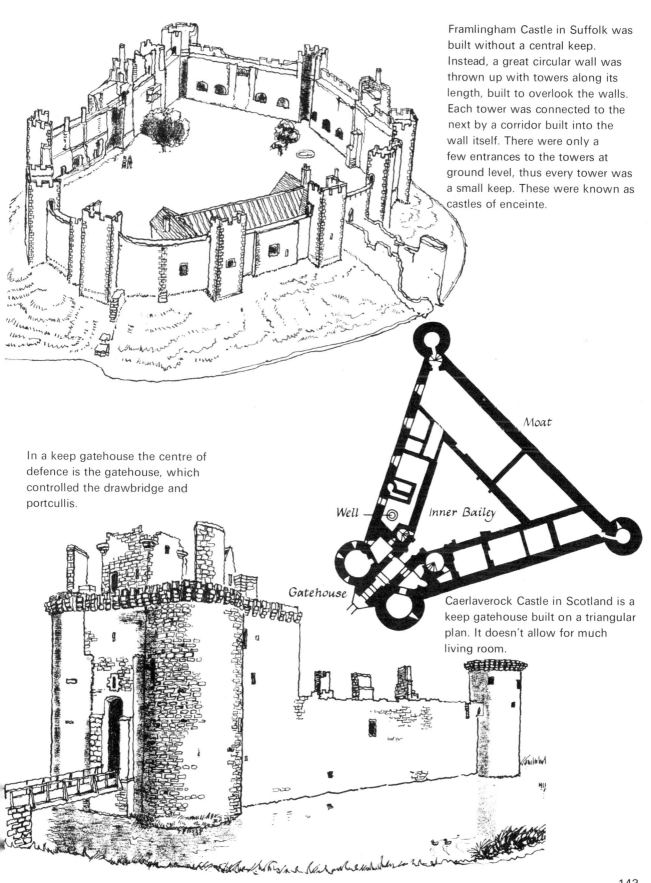

Framlingham Castle in Suffolk was built without a central keep. Instead, a great circular wall was thrown up with towers along its length, built to overlook the walls. Each tower was connected to the next by a corridor built into the wall itself. There were only a few entrances to the towers at ground level, thus every tower was a small keep. These were known as castles of enceinte.

In a keep gatehouse the centre of defence is the gatehouse, which controlled the drawbridge and portcullis.

Moat

Well — Inner Bailey

Gatehouse

Caerlaverock Castle in Scotland is a keep gatehouse built on a triangular plan. It doesn't allow for much living room.

The development of castles in the reign of Edward I owed much to knowledge gained in the Crusades.

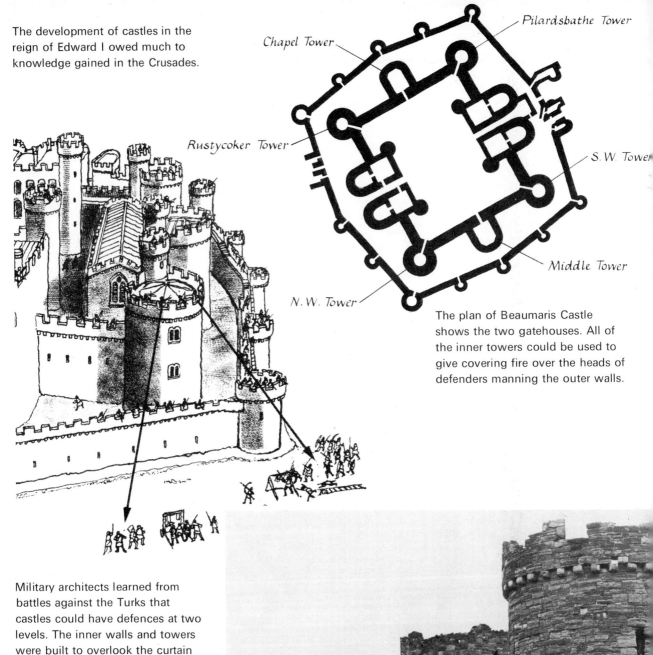

Chapel Tower

Pilardsbathe Tower

Rustycoker Tower

S.W. Tower

N.W. Tower

Middle Tower

The plan of Beaumaris Castle shows the two gatehouses. All of the inner towers could be used to give covering fire over the heads of defenders manning the outer walls.

Military architects learned from battles against the Turks that castles could have defences at two levels. The inner walls and towers were built to overlook the curtain wall and its towers. All the ground in front of the castle was thus covered from above. This is known as a concentric castle.

The curtain wall of Beaumaris Castle in Anglesey looks unassailable even today. It was built by the architect to Edward I, Master James of St George.

Edward I built a string of stone castles across Wales, including Harlech. Here, at Harlech Castle, Gwynnedd, the plan is based on a square.

Until the 1400s castles had been built of stone. The final phase of castle building saw the use of brick, as here at Tattershall Castle, Lincolnshire. It was built between 1434 and 1446.

Another famous brick built castle is Hurstmonceux Castle in Sussex. Gunpowder influenced the construction of castles. They developed into houses for the lord, with walls around which defenders could move with ease. These later castles have gun ports, or holes.

145

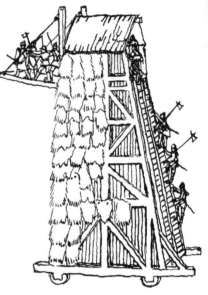

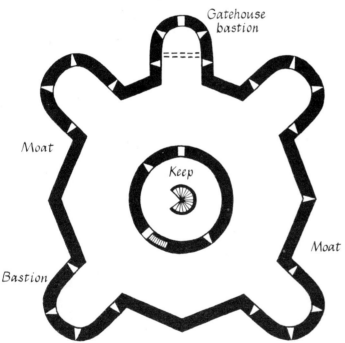

Gatehouse
bastion

Moat

Keep

Moat

Bastion

Henry VIII built the last series of castles in England. They were shaped rather like a flower and were used to house guns to protect the coast from invasion. At the centre were the living quarters for the garrison, and an ammunition store. This plan and picture is of Camber Castle, Sussex.

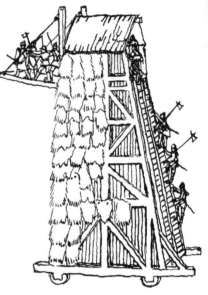

A siege tower was wheeled up to the walls by attackers.

A battering ram.

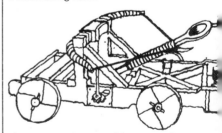

A mangonel was a big catapult.

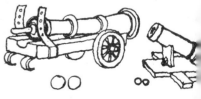

Some early cannon.

UNDER

SIEGE

A sappers' tent. They dug under the foundations, then burned the supports.

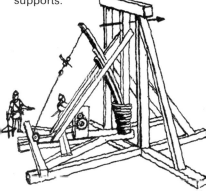

The ballista was used to throw stones and arrows against the castle.

A protective shield on wheels was called a mantlet.

Corfe Castle, Dorset, was bravely defended by Lady Bankes for Charles I but it was almost totally destroyed by the Parliamentarians. After the end of the Civil War Oliver Cromwell ordered many castles to be 'slighted'—or so flattened by gunpowder that they could never be used in war again.

Corfe Castle as it is today with the quiet village below.

Norm

The barbican was a defensive tower before the main gatehouse, as here at Carisbrooke Castle, Isle of Wight.

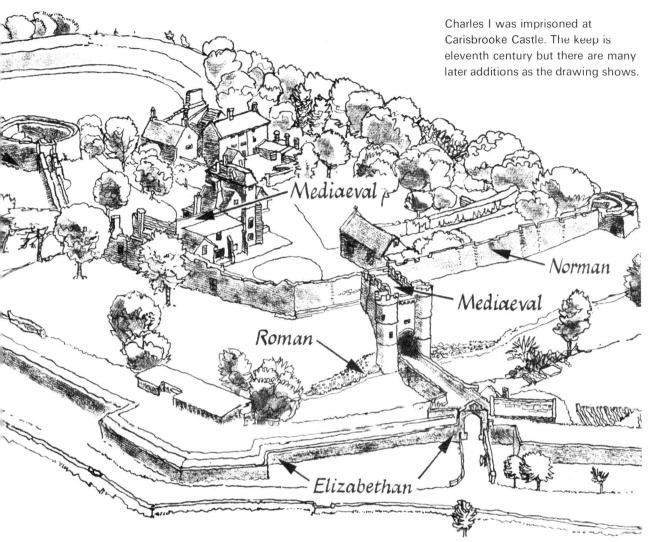

Charles I was imprisoned at Carisbrooke Castle. The keep is eleventh century but there are many later additions as the drawing shows.

Mediaeval

Norman

Mediaeval

Roman

Elizabethan

MILITARY FEATURES

The north platform and bastion towers of Caerphilly Castle, Glamorganshire, show the oubliettes, or pits in the wall behind each tower. They were once covered by pivoted trapdoors operated by a garrison in retreat.

The inner ward and flanking towers
of White Castle, Monmouth, viewed
across the moat.

A gatehouse door with its wooden
bolt in position.

A drawbridge was often raised by
counterpoise. The weights were
housed inside the tower. The wooden
beams are called rainures.

At Caldicot Castle gatehouse, Gwent, the portcullis is raised. Many gatehouses had both a drawbridge and a portcullis. In the ceiling are murder holes through which arrows could be fired on unwelcome visitors.

The gatehouse tower of Raglan Castle is machicolated. Through the holes defenders dropped missiles on their enemies.

The crossbow was used in confined spaces—like castle towers.

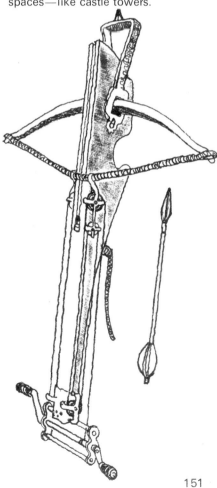

Arrow slits, or loop-holes, provided a good view for the archer while offering maximum protection. On the left is an arrow slit in Marten's Tower, Chepstow. On the right, an arrow slit has been converted to a gun port at the base, in the Great Tower at Raglan, Gwent.

A newel staircase gave the defending knight an advantage in hand-to-hand combat.

The walls of a castle varied in thickness. An angled, and therefore thicker, base, made the wall more difficult to mine. The pathway along the top of the wall is called an allure walk. This parapet and walk is on the middle bailey south wall, Chepstow.

Sometimes the walls of the castle adjoined the town walls. An outer defensive wall beyond the curtain wall was called the mantlet. This shows the town walls at Conway.

DOMESTIC FEATURES

Meat was roasted on an open fire, turned on a spit — a thin pointed rod. This might be turned by hand, or by a dog whose movements would turn the wheel. This is a dog-turned spit.

The sink at Orford Castle drains through the wall to a spout outside.

Castles were places in which people lived, as well as being fortresses in time of war. There were kitchens and living quarters. The Great Hall at Stokesay Castle, Shropshire, looks cold and bare, but once the Lord and his family and friends were comfortable here.

Two sixteenth century fireplaces on Chepstow's lower bailey.

The well in the courtyard of Goodrich Castle, Herefordshire.

A chimney pot at Grosmont Castle, Gwent.

A mural gallery ran round the inside of the keep. This one is Norman.

This mural gallery is Gothic.

A sculpted quatrefoil stone at Caldicot Castle, Gwent, shows the name of the castle's fourteenth century builder—Thomas, for Thomas Woodstock.

A chapel might be built within the keep or gatehouse, or it might be a separate building. The Round Chapel, Ludlow Castle, Shropshire, is Norman.

The stone-carved hunting horn on a chimney at St Briavels Castle, Gloucestershire, indicates its former use as a royal hunting lodge.

This heraldic carved canopy is over a state bedroom window in Raglan Castle, Gwent.

The piscina and a sedilia in the chapel at Caerphilly Castle.

Prison wall graffito in St Briavels Castle, Gloucestershire, brings the past to life. It reads, 'Wilam Bound was takn 11 off June 1677'.

A Romanesque arcade in the Great Tower, Chepstow. The two round windows were added later, probably for ventilation.

RAILWAYS

It comes as something of a shock to learn that railways did not begin in 1825 when the first train ran between Stockton and Darlington, and that George Stephenson did not design the first locomotive. But the facts speak for themselves.

The technique of moving coal trucks from pit head to navigable water was used by miners in Tyneside and Nottinghamshire as early as 1650. By 1700 these trucks on wooden rails were called a 'Newcastle road'. Later in the century, when iron rails began to be cast at Coalbrookdale, metal replaced wood. At this stage men and animals, not machines, moved the trucks.

Parallel with this development were attempts to use steam as a source of power. Thomas Newcomen, in 1712, and James Watt, in 1769, had developed stationary steam-driven engines which were suitable for pumping water from mines. A steam engine that moved however, posed almost insurmountable difficulties. William Murdoch made a model engine in 1784. This worked reasonably well and caused the vicar of Redruth to flee from its path when he saw it moving slowly towards him down the road. The steam, smoke and smell, he remarked later, led him to believe that the engine was actually a re-incarnation of the Devil.

The real father of the modern railroad was Richard Trevithick who, in 1804, built a steam engine for the Penydarren Ironworks near Merthyr Tydfil in South Wales. It was sufficiently powerful to haul ten tons of iron a distance of nine miles at a speed of 5 mph. However the engine was not really successful. It proved too heavy for

the rails which it repeatedly broke. The owners took off its wheels and used it as a stationary engine.

Although Trevithick's engine was something of a failure, the observation made by a reporter on its first journey is prophetic: 'The number of horses in the kingdom will be very considerably reduced and the machine made use of in a

thousand instances never yet thought of.' In 1813, William Hedley, a Northumberland engineer, built the most famous locomotive of all—'Puffing Billy'.

And so we come to George Stephenson. He was born in Wylam near Newcastle, the very village in which William Hedley's 'Puffing Billy' was built. Stephenson came of a mining family, and he followed his father into the colliery but not to the pit face. He became an engine-wright. His first successful locomotive was completed in 1814. Named after the Prussian general, 'Blücher', it could pull 30 tons of coal at a speed of 4 mph.

George Stephenson's influence on the development of the railways was profound. In 1821 he persuaded Edward Pease, a local landowner, to built a railway between Stockton and Darlington and to lay the line on the assumption that steam locomotives would be used to haul the trucks. On September 25, 1825, the railway opened. As the *Durham County Advertiser* reported: 'Astonishment was not confined to human species for the beasts of the field and the fowls of the air seemed to view with wonder and awe the machine which now moved onward at a rate of 10–12 mph with a weight of not less than 80 tons attached to it.' A railway boom did not immediately follow: the Liverpool and Manchester Railway (1826–30) was something of a failure. But after 1830 railways spread like a rash. By 1855 seven thousand miles of working track criss-crossed the country.

The effect on travelling time was nothing short of amazing. In 1754 it had taken $4\frac{1}{2}$ days to reach Manchester from London; in 1838 it took only 12 hours.

The birth of the railways gave mobility to the population. Far more people could travel—for holidays, for work, for pleasure, and entertainment—and raw materials, consumer goods, foodstuffs and mail could be moved across the country cheaply, quickly and safely.

We have come a long way since 'Puffing Billy', 'Blücher' and 'Rocket'. One national railway company has replaced the multitude of tiny lines of Victorian Britain. We are closing lines instead of opening them, and we no longer marvel at trains which travel ten times as fast as 'locomotion'.

Before the railway companies joined together in 1923, every company chose its own coat of arms. These stained glass windows show the coat of arms of the North Staffordshire Railway.

One way to recapture the past world of railways is to visit a railway museum. Engines from the last century have been restored, and are housed where they can be comfortably examined, to serve as reminders of the romantic age of steam travel. The London and South Western Railway Locomotive No 363.

The old railway companies have now ceased to exist, but examples of their arms and emblems can be found tucked away in odd corners of railway stations. This old East Lancashire Railway coat of arms was cast in iron and mounted on the gates of Bury station. Though the gates have been pulled down the arms can now be seen in the booking hall.

The Great Western Railway's initials have been used here as part of the design for a platform seat. Decorative monograms such as this were frequently used.

The Stockton to Darlington Railway opened in 1825 and ushered in a new era. George Stephenson, 'the father of railways', was chosen to take charge of the building. The Darlington coat of arms shows a picture of Stephenson's famous engine which he built for the line.

George Stephenson's birthplace— Street House, Wylam, near Newcastle.
The 'Rocket', built by George Stephenson and his son Robert won a competition and became the chosen locomotive for the new Liverpool to Manchester line.

The coat of arms of Crewe has a railway wheel with six spokes representing the six important routes for which Crewe is a junction.

William Hedley was an engineer who had been inspired by Richard Trevithick's steam engine. Hedley's 'Puffing Billy' can be seen today at the Science Museum, London.

The crest of the Great Central Railway was created in 1897.

George Stephenson built the 'North Star' in 1837 for the New Orleans Railway of America. It was bought instead by the Great Western Railway, and hauled the first passenger train from Paddington to Maidenhead in 1838.

Old railway company boundary sign.

A well-known engine in the Railway Museum at York is the GNR No 1, built in Doncaster in 1870 by another famous engineer, Patrick Stirling.

The railways created whole new towns and holiday resorts. Towns which the railways by-passed were at a disadvantage. The railway changed the face of Stockport in Cheshire when this great viaduct was built through the centre of the town.

In 1904 an engine was built which could travel at over 100 mph. This was the 'City of Truro', built at Swindon in 1903, and reputed to have reached a speed of 102.3 mph.

The railways provided work for the people who built them, who ran them and for those who supplied the necessary building materials. Difficult building feats were accomplished, as the building of the cutting at Tring, Hertfordshire, on the London and Birmingham Railway, which dates from 1834.

RAILWAY STATIONS

Stone and brick were used. English bond brickwork is alternate layers of 'stretchers', the side, and 'headers', the end.

Flemish bond uses alternate headers and stretchers in each layer.

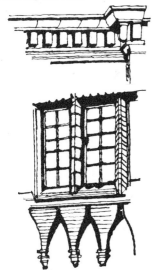

Bricks of different colours were used together to create a pattern or were moulded to give patterns.

Differently shaped pieces of stone might be used. Above, corner-stones are found on both brick and stone buildings.

A variety of styles were used for doorways and entrances.

The Royal Porch, Windsor and Eton Riverside Station.

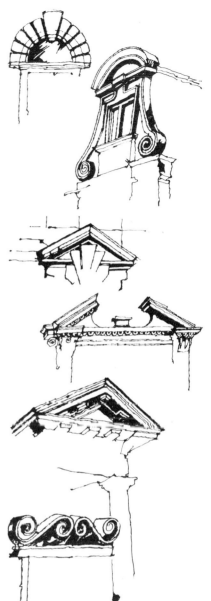

Classical pediments and shaped windows.

Harleston Station, Norfolk, has the look of a large town house.

Curzon Street station, built in 1837, in Birmingham, is grand in the classical style. It was the original terminus of the London–Birmingham line.

Station buildings vary enormously in style and size. They might be impressively classical, reflecting the influence of Greece, or the Italian Renaissance; some were designed like country cottages; some were built like cathedrals in the Gothic style; and of course there are modern stations. This station at Chester was designed by the architect Francis Thompson in 1848.

Audley End porte-cochère.

There is a great deal of variety in roofs and walls. Contrasting tiles, unusual gables and decorated bargeboards are all to be found.

A cupola and dormer window at Thornton Heath Station, Surrey.

Attractive ironwork and weathervane top the station at Boxhill and West Humble Station, Surrey.

The windows at Battle Station in Sussex.

Stoke on Trent Station presents an
interesting Flemish-style facade.

A date mark in diaper work, the
use of coloured bricks to create a
pattern, is at Windsor and Eton
Riverside Station.

The station at Fenny Stratford
was designed to look like a Tudor
cottage, with black and white
timber walling, and carved
bargeboards.

Euston Station colonnade is modern in design.

Wolverhampton Station.

During the nineteenth century a number of stations were designed which resembled Gothic cathedrals. When St Pancras Station in London was completed in 1874 everyone thought it was the greatest building of the railway age. Because the station was built during the reign of Queen Victoria the style is called Victorian Gothic.

A wooden veranda was built on the first Manchester station in 1830.

The platform covering of St Pancras Station, built in 1865, was magnificent to look at even though its only function was to protect trains and passengers from the weather.

Verandas may have decorated edgings, or pelmets, called valances. Some platform covering are attached to the building with brackets as at Frant Station, Sussex.

Loughton Station, Essex, has a cantilevered platform veranda, a design made possible by the use of steel and concrete.

The verandas at Holywell Junction, Flintshire, are supported at each end of the station building with jutting-out bays.

A station clock was installed in the booking hall at Gravesend Town Pier in 1834 but it was later transferred to Barking Station. From 1961 it has been on display in the Museum of British Transport.

Cast iron and wrought iron came into use because these materials were stronger than wood. Lots of early stations have verandas supported on cast-iron pillars. This decorated cast-iron column is from Dorking Station, Surrey.

The letterbox at Ruabon Station dates from the reign of Queen Victoria.

A helpful cupid at Liverpool Street Station is shown stoking a boiler. Decorations can be surprisingly fanciful.

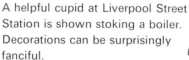

Details on these decorated valances vary tremendously in shape and style.

RAILWAY ENGINEERING

Until recently 67,000 bridges were in use on British Rail. The most common types are beam bridges, which go straight across, and arch bridges, like this one at Kearsley, Lancashire.

A viaduct is really a long arch-type bridge. This disused one is the viaduct at Ingleton, Yorkshire.

Cantilever bridges are quite rare. The Forth Railway Bridge in Scotland is cantilever design.

Suspension bridges are also rare. This is the Royal Albert Bridge at Saltash, Cornwall.

Most bridges cross over the line at right-angles to the road or river. Skew bridges, such as this one at Bath Spa Station, cross at an oblique angle.

A castellated viaduct at Bath spa Station looks more like the entrance to a castle.

Tunnels were expensive and difficult to make. This is the entrance to Red Hill Tunnel, south of the River Trent.

Another less usual type of bridge is a movable bridge. This one is the Hawarden Swing Bridge in Clwyd.

A cutting near Chorley in Lancashire has flying arches to stop the banks of the cutting from falling in.

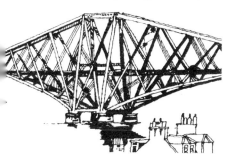

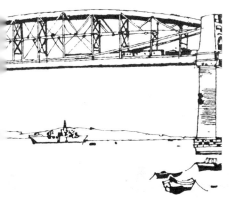

Some cuttings were carved out of solid rock while others needed supporting walls. This brick arcading is in the cutting at North Dulwich, London.

ON THE LINE

There are about two thousand level crossings used by the general public.

On busy lines signals are mounted on a bracket like this one.

Signals can be mounted on a gantry.

Drivers of LARGE or SLOW VEHICLES must phone and get permission to cross

LARGE means over 55' long or 9'6" wide or 32 tons total weight
SLOW means 5mph or less

Safe height 16'6"

AUTOMATIC BARRIERS STOP when lights show

Uneven Crossing Risk of grounding

These are some of the signs to be seen at level crossings.

Most railway lines are fenced off.

These posts mark the distance from the last mile post.

These are shunting signals.

A gradient post indicates the slope.

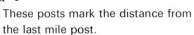

Speed restrictions are clearly marked.

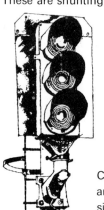
Colour light signals are like traffic signals.

CANALS

As we travel across Britain along smooth roads or in the comfort of a modern train, it's easy to regard the canal builders as mere eccentrics. Many canals which once carried vital goods between town and factory are now little more than brackish backwaters, and those that are still functional seem designed more to meet the needs of the holidaymaker than those of industry.

One needs to imagine a time when our roads were not smooth and well kept and there were no commercial railroads. Imagine trying to move heavy goods—coal, iron, or one of those new fangled pumping engines—by packhorse along a muddy road in winter. Even worse, imagine moving the delicate porcelain ware of Derby and Staffordshire by cart along hard rutted roads in the height of a dry summer. Industry could not expand and develop if the raw materials it needed, or the goods it produced, could not be moved.

Waterways had, of course, from time immemorial been used for transport—but it was not always convenient, or possible, to build factories by rivers.

Even when the roads were improved the tolls charged were often so high as to make the regular movement of goods along them uneconomic. The solution lay in waterborne transport. Where there were no rivers let there be canals.

The first commercial canal was opened in 1757, to transport coal between St. Helens and the Mersey (near Warrington). It is overshadowed in our history books by a canal built by the Duke of Bridgewater who was granted the right, by Act of Parliament, to link his coal mines in Worsley to Manchester. A canal, only ten miles in length, would cut the price of coal in Manchester by half! The scheme was an ambitious one. It involved cutting a tunnel to take the canal into the mines, as well as the building of an aqueduct to carry it over the River Irwell. The engineer in charge was James Brindley. When the canal was opened in 1761 it foreshadowed the canal age.

The most perceptive supporter of these first canals was Josiah Wedgwood, whose potteries were dependent upon reliable and efficient transport. His support was both political and financial. Despite considerable opposition from landowners, Wedgwood, and other entrepreneurs like him, led a movement which saw canals spread across the country.

A whole new technology developed in the process from the cutting of tunnels to the building of aqueducts; from fashioning water-tight locks to building bridges and barges. The skill of the canal engineers can be appreciated even today. The idea of taking a canal across the Pennines is breathtaking in itself; to actually build a canal from Leeds to Liverpool, a major feat of engineering in any age! It is fair to observe that the route chosen was somewhat circuitous (127 miles) and that it took 46 years to build. But its opening, in 1816, perhaps marks the peak of the canal engineers' skill.

Canal development also had the effect of creating new centres of population. People and the services

they provided would congregate at canal junctions. Birmingham became the focal point of canal communication linking the Black country with London, Worcester, Bristol, Lancashire and Yorkshire. Although Birmingham was an industrial centre before the coming of the canals, its subsequent rapid expansion can be attributed more to canal development than to any other factor.

No parts of the British mainland escaped the canal developers. In the South the Thames was linked to the Severn, in Scotland the Forth to the Clyde. In Wales the Ellesmere canal involved the construction of the two most famous aqueducts of all—at Pontcysyllte and Chirk.

When wandering along the banks of a canal—whether it is still working or not—it's fun to 'collect' the odd and unusual. Warehouses, the decoration on the barges, strange pieces of machinery, such as sluice gear, lock cottages, toll houses, tunnel and bridge keepers houses, indicate how sophisticated this method of transport became— before it was eclipsed for ever by rail, road and motorway.

A disused wharf and overgrown canal stand as reminders of a busy past.

Some canals continue to be used and some have been restored for recreational purposes. The canal age stretched from 1759 to 1850 when railways took over. Now restoration is taking place, as at this lock keeper's house.

Originally a working canal boat was pulled by a gang of men or by horse, mule or donkey. Nowadays the few that exist are diesel driven. Narrow boats, made of wood and sometimes of steel, were twenty-one metres long by two metres wide. Usually the leading boat was drawn by a horse, and towed the 'butty' boat behind. This one is diesel driven.

Canals which once were derelict and unsafe can be revitalised. The Rochdale Canal, Manchester (above), was landscaped and rebuilt to provide a new leisure area (below).

Locks were used whenever the canal had to go uphill or downhill. Boats enter at one level and pass through a series of gates until free water is reached. This disused flight of locks is on the Kennet and Avon Canal.

CANAL BUILDINGS

These old canalside cottages once housed the warehousemen and boatmen.

The Gas Street Basin is in the heart of Birmingham. Working narrow boats of the Birmingham & Midland Canal Company are on the right, while on the left are narrow boats which have been converted into floating homes and holiday cruisers.

An iron wall support of an old canal building.

A toll house was used by the toll clerks who collected tolls from the boatmen who used the canal. This one is octagonal.

This lighthouse served the entrance to the Caledonian Canal in Scotland.

Many canal buildings are past repair, but this warehouse is still being used.

Some bridges had a bridge keeper who lived next to the bridge.

This bridge keeper's house was built rather grandly in classical style.

The lock keeper lived next to his lock and many of the old cottages remain, as here on the Chester Canal.

These old houses in Lincoln were built over the canal. The bridge underneath is known as the 'Glory Hole'.

Working and pleasure boats at a boat-builder's yard.

Tunnels were difficult and dangerous to build, and sometimes took years to complete. A disused house stands like a sentry above the Braunston Tunnel on the Grand Union Canal.

Alongside this bridge, carefully concealed, is a concrete pillbox. It was built during the last war to defend the bridge when invasion threatened.

Inns and public houses were built everywhere along the canal, usually near towns and villages, to provide for canal workers, boatmen and passengers as their names clearly indicate.

The rudder of an old barge makes an unusual sign for this pub. Relics of the past such as this, and the interesting locations of canal-side pubs make them very interesting to visit.

This public house is on a ship canal. A pilot was necessary to direct a large boat out into an otherwise dangerous river.

LOCKS

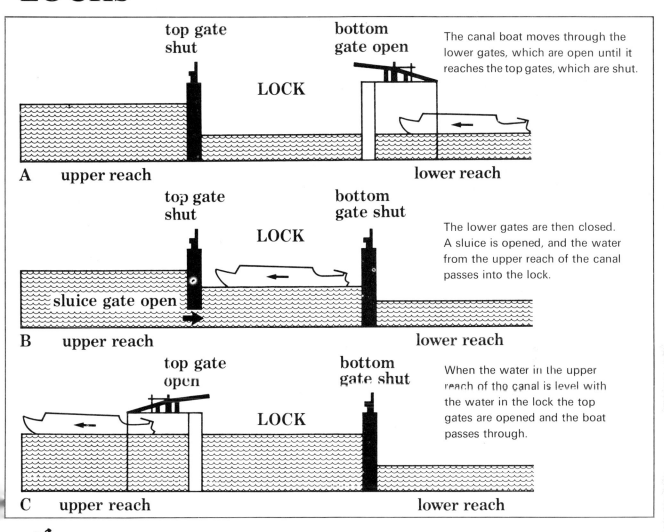

A   upper reach

top gate shut   bottom gate open   LOCK   lower reach

The canal boat moves through the lower gates, which are open until it reaches the top gates, which are shut.

B   upper reach

top gate shut   bottom gate shut   LOCK   sluice gate open   lower reach

The lower gates are then closed. A sluice is opened, and the water from the upper reach of the canal passes into the lock.

C   upper reach

top gate open   bottom gate shut   LOCK   lower reach

When the water in the upper reach of the canal is level with the water in the lock the top gates are opened and the boat passes through.

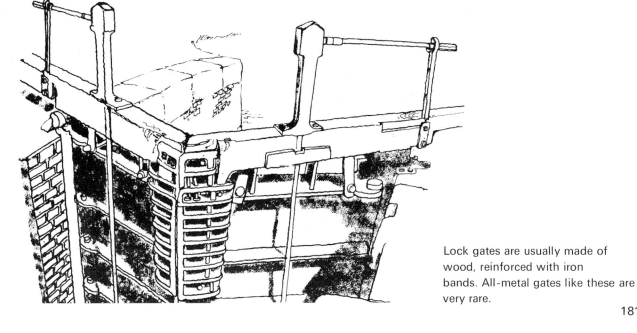

Lock gates are usually made of wood, reinforced with iron bands. All-metal gates like these are very rare.

The heavy balance beam was numbered on the underside with the lock number.

Narrow boats, laden with coal, are ascending the three locks, Soulbury, on the Grand Union Canal near Leighton Buzzard.

The sluice gate is operated by a ratchet, which is attached to the sluice gate below.

Some gates have foot bridges or handrails fixed on to them.

The Anderton lift, built in 1874, lifts boats from the River Weaver to the Trent and Mersey Canal. Lifts were sometimes used to save the trouble of building locks.

Stones or bricks set into the ground follow the line of the swing of the balance beam to give sure footing for the operator.

A stop lock is mainly used when the difference in levels between the canals on either side of the lock is only a few inches. Others were built to take tolls.

TUNNELS, BRIDGES & AQUEDUCTS

One way to avoid building a flight of locks to carry the canal over a hill was to make a tunnel through it. There are about fifty canal tunnels in Britain, including the Sapperton Tunnel on the Thames and Severn Canal.

The most common type of bridge over a canal was hump-backed.

Most early tunnels had no towpath so instead of pulling the boat through by horse it was often 'legged' through by a man on each side.

Other types of bridges can be found, such as this pointed arch bridge.

An arched bridge with a stone balustrade at Newbury in Berkshire.

This bridge carries the M1 Motorway over a canal. Modern building materials give it an entirely different look from the old stone bridges.

Thomas Telford built this tall arched bridge on the Shropshire Union Canal.

Cast iron bridges such as this one are quite rare. The name of the iron founders can often be found on the bridge.

The construction of a roving bridge made it possible for a towing horse to cross over from one bank to the other without unhitching.

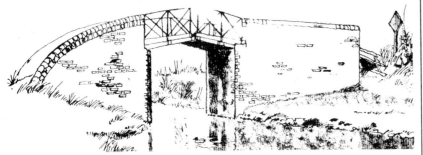

A split or divided bridge allowed the tow-rope to slip through the gap without having to be cast off and refastened.

A swing bridge can be swung open from one side of the bank to another, or swung open from an island in the middle. This wooden swing bridge is across the entrance to a repairing dock.

Bridge numbers and names are often found on or near a bridge. Most bridges have a canal company number, usually on a cast-iron plate above the arch. Sometimes the number is in Roman numerals.

A road swing bridge.

An aqueduct was built whenever the canal had to pass over a road, a river, or a deep valley. The most famous one is the Pontcysyllte Aqueduct that carries the Ellesmere Canal over the River Dee near Llangollen in North Wales. It was built by Thomas Telford in 1803.

A lift bridge, or bascule bridge, can be raised and lowered like a castle drawbridge.

Telford's aqueduct passes over the Holyhead road (now the A5). The road was also built by Telford.

Mile posts were used to tell the boatmen how far it was to the next town or junction, and also to help him and the tollkeeper calculate the toll charge.

Though most of the canal is now disused, this pumping station is still maintained in working order by the Kennet and Avon Canal Trust Ltd.

Signposts were used to point the way at canal junctions.

Some bollards and mooring rings are deeply rope-worn.

RIVERS

To follow a river from its source to the sea would have been something of a major expedition in Victorian times. Today, should we wish to do so, we could follow the Thames from the Cotswolds to the Essex marshes in a few hours motoring. The car has opened up the countryside. In one day the modern family can visit places miles apart.

wash the fleeces of sheep. Tanners, sadlers, cordwainers, bottle makers and paper makers needed water just as much as ship builders, sail makers, farmers and fruit growers. This competition for water has not decreased with the passage of time. The popularity of water sports, the increasing consumption of water in home and factory, its use in the production of electric power has made conservation of this natural asset more important today than ever before in our history.

But to cross the Thames at Woolwich and the Humber at New Holland it is still necessary to travel by boat. The ferry may be driven by propeller, if the route is straightforward; paddle, if tight turns are required; or chain, if the distance between the river banks is comparatively narrow.

Our rivers are not as rich in shipping as they once were. The red-sailed Thames barge is now little more than a museum piece, and many of our once busy inland ports have declined in importance with the advent of ships of ever increasing tonnage. But the decline of our inland ports has not been all loss. Our rivers are cleaner and the reduction of pollution has meant that wild life has returned—ducks and water birds to marshland, sea trout and salmon to rivers they last used for breeding four hundred years ago.

Rivers, of course, have played a very important part in our economic development. If rivers were navigable it meant that goods could be transported along them—and the fact that seventeen acts of Parliament relating to the improvement of rivers were passed between 1662–1700 underlines the vital part they played in the industrial life of the country. By 1700, over 1,000 miles of river were regularly used for transport and very few towns of any importance lay more than 20 miles from a navigable waterway.

Our use of water has been far from haphazard. To the river's edge have come brewers in search of water pure enough to make beer and whisky, millers who harnessed the speed of its flow to turn water wheels to grind their corn, and fullers who needed soft water to

Rivers also present a natural barrier to the traveller. Down the centuries they have had to be crossed—by stepping stone or ford; by simple clapper bridge; by bridges made from wood, stone, brick, iron and steel; bridges that are fixed; bridges that open; bridges so low that a canoeist would find them impassible; bridges so high that a great ship can pass through them with ease. Around them have grown towns, upon them have been erected houses to collect tolls and chapels in which to say prayers.

Where bridges could not be built, ferries, many of them long-established, have been used to take people and their goods across the water. Queen's Ferry, near Edinburgh, which was so named because of its royal connections, has been replaced by a bridge.

The river bank, whether the river runs through reclaimed industrial wasteland or country valley, is a place to explore. For, as it moves from countryside to sea, the river in all its moods and changes of scenery echoes the changing face of Britain—farming community, rural hamlet, industrial town, deep sea port. The very names of the places along its length often comment on its path—Kempsford, Carswell Marsh, Oxford, Wallingford, Goring Gap, Weybridge, Brentford, Isle of Dogs, Greenhithe, Thames Haven, Southend-on-Sea.

Down the centuries the rivers have flowed to the sea, a thought which has led many a poet to use images of the river to illustrate human life from birth to death. The writer of the book of *Proverbs* was even more profound in remarking that 'although all the rivers run into the sea it is not full'.

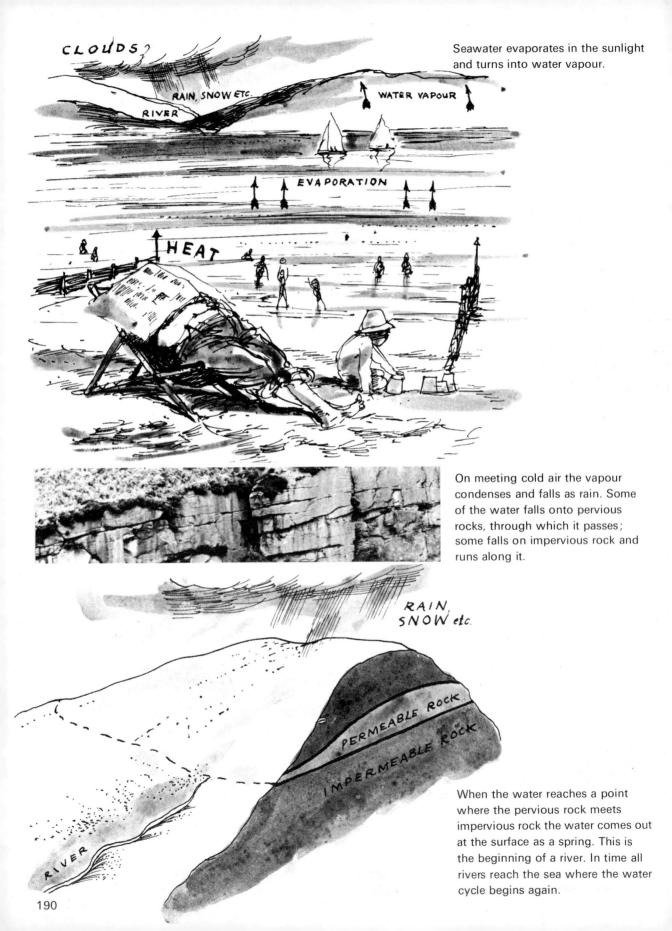

CLOUDS?

Seawater evaporates in the sunlight and turns into water vapour.

RAIN, SNOW ETC.

RIVER

WATER VAPOUR

EVAPORATION

HEAT

On meeting cold air the vapour condenses and falls as rain. Some of the water falls onto pervious rocks, through which it passes; some falls on impervious rock and runs along it.

RAIN, SNOW etc.

PERMEABLE ROCK

IMPERMEABLE ROCK

RIVER

When the water reaches a point where the pervious rock meets impervious rock the water comes out at the surface as a spring. This is the beginning of a river. In time all rivers reach the sea where the water cycle begins again.

The banks of the river and the river bed wear away as the river gathers momentum. The river makes a valley shaped like the letter V. The land that juts out is called a spur. When several spurs fit together like this they are described as interlocking.

There are four stages in the life story of a river. At first the water flows very slowly. After a mile or two it travels more swiftly and more water reaches it from small tributary streams. The River Wharfe.

Swiftly moving water can cut through rock and carry large boulders downstream. This material increases its power to wear away the banks.

After days of heavy rain there is even more foam, froth and swirling water. The river is in spate. The river Wharfe in spate under Burnsall Bridge has overflowed.

As boulders are whirled round by swiftly moving water they gouge holes in the river bottom called rock pools.

The tremendous energy of a river is also shown in flooding. Here the River Wye in flood at Brockweir, Gloucestershire, has marooned a Land Rover.

The Strid is a channel only a few feet wide but very deep where the River Wharfe has cut through the rock.

There may also be waterfalls in the second stage of a river. Soft rock is worn away more quickly leaving the hard rock protruding which the water flows over, forming a waterfall. Where there are several strips of hard rock a series of small waterfalls, or rapids, is formed. This is Thornton Force, Yorkshire.

Gordale Beck runs through a deep gorge, known as Gordale Scar, to reach the River Aire. The cliffs rise to over 90 metres on each side.

Pecca Falls, near Ingleton, Yorkshire.

A waterfall can be formed in three ways. In the illustration above, the black areas represent hard rock that water cannot wear away quickly.

The point at which the river disappears is called a water sink or swallow hole. The river flows into underground holes. Gaping Gill is one of the best known of these potholes.

Scalebar Force, Yorkshire.

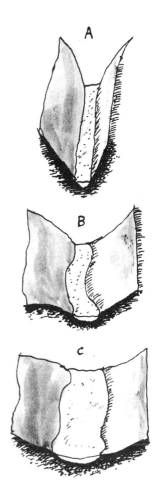

In time, the energy of the river seems to become less. In its middle stage it moves more slowly and carries sand and mud. This is the silt that it deposits on the riverbed.

At certain times of the year a high tide, called a bore, may roll up some rivers from the sea. The Severn bore is shown here.

195

A river wears away its banks, sometimes one bank more than another. It can also wear away the underbank so that it overhangs.

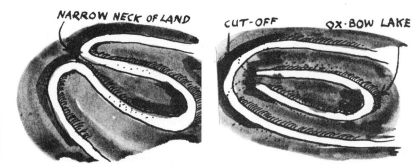

NARROW NECK OF LAND   CUT-OFF   OX·BOW LAKE

A meandering river may eventually form an 'ox-bow' lake.

In the last stage of the river it wanders, or meanders, across a plain. When flooding takes place mud is spread over the ground.

A river may wear away the bank and expose tree roots until eventually the tree topples over.

Large stones are deposited near the middle of a river, smaller ones near the edge.

Near the source of a river there may be a floodgate to trap debris.

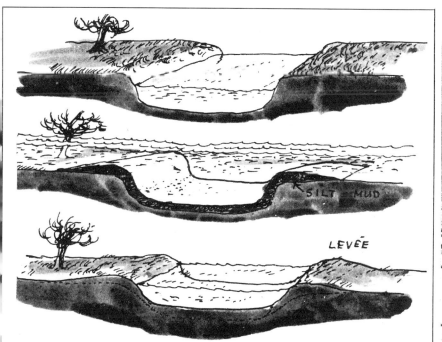

SILT — MUD

LEVÉE

Raised river banks, levees, are formed when a river floods and deposits layers of mud and silt on the banks. In time these become covered with grass and form new raised banks.

A flood indicator shows the speed at which the river is rising in time of heavy rain.

A river estuary with the tide out. At high tide the water would reach the top level of the darker wood on the standing piles.

When the river deposits silt the river bed becomes filled and may require dredging. Mud is lifted into barges and dumped at sea.

LONG REACH

USING RIVERS

BREWING

CORNLANDS

SHEEP GRAZE

WEAVING + FULLING SHEDS

WOOL DRESSING (TALLOW)

SOAP BOILERS

CHANDLERS

BEES WAX → REFUSE

FRUIT & VEGETABLES

FLAX →

BUILDING & BASKET WILLOWS

HEMP

RETTING PONDS

ROPE WORKS

ESTUARY

CORN MILLS CITY

MARKET

SLAUGHTER-HOUSE

SKINNERS

BONE YARD

LEATHER VATS

HORN WORKS

GLUE BOILERS

REFUSE DUMPS

POTASH PITS

SMALL FISHING BOATYARDS

WASTE WOOD - TAR

FISH SMOKING + CURING SHEDS

THATCH REEDS

WILD FOWL

SALTINGS

FLOW

From the earliest days of history people have made use of rivers. A river valley provided good soil, water, a means of travel, and a way to dispose of waste. A brewery would be erected near the source of a river where the water was clean; corn mills needed swiftly running water to turn the mill wheels; near the meadows were the woollen industry's fulling mills; lower down were rope works. The tanners were near the cattle market. For everyone the river meant transport.

199

The water mill at Skenfrith, Gwent. Some mills have been converted into attractive homes, others have been left to collapse.

Coracles were small round boats made of leather stretched round a wicker framework. They are known as curraghs in Ireland where they are still used. They are also common in parts of Wales.

The old water wheel at Skenfrith.

HAMMERS LIFTED BY TRIPS

PIVOT

TRIP

WHEEL TURNED BY MILL WHEEL

Fulling is a process in the woollen industry in which the cloth is soaked in soapy water and beaten with very heavy wooden hammers, called mallets. This is to clean and shrink the cloth.

Fishing, or angling, is popular in some areas, and some streams are specially stocked with fish.

Here, the Dinas dam is part of the Rheidol hydroelectric scheme in Wales. Building a dam is a way of harnessing a river's energy.

At low tide in the Severn Estuary the shrimpers come out with their nets.

A canoe or kayak can be tricky to manoeuvre.

A Thames River Police launch.

Buckler's Hard, Hampshire, became an important ship building centre. The Master Builder's House stands by the Beaulieu River.

A four-oar racing boat.

Littlehampton Harbour is on a river estuary.

BRIDGES

A shallow place in a river, called a ford, was used for crossing.

A wooden beam bridge near Ingleton, Yorkshire.

The Albert suspension Bridge, one of the prettiest in London, was built in 1873.

A clapper bridge, at Malham, Yorkshire, with stone supports in the river.

Waterloo Bridge relies upon supports too but is rather more streamlined.

A ferry is another way to cross.

To build an arch bridge, a framework of wood was first made across the river. Then wedge-shaped stones were built side by side to the crown. When the last piece was in place the framework was removed. This packhorse bridge is so-called because it was probably paid for by travelling pedlars.

A chapel built on to a bridge in Wakefield, South Yorkshire. There are only three chapels on bridges in Britain.

The piles of stone for supports eventually became pillars, or piers. If angles were built on these they lessened the pressure of the water. Also, they could make alcoves on the road in which people could stand to let traffic pass. This bridge is at Ilkley, Yorkshire.

SEACOAST

The sea has played a rather special part in our history as a nation. All around our coast can be seen evidence of man's struggle to master the sea. For centuries, our ships have traded along the sea routes of the world, the oceans have been harvested to bring us fish whilst drilling the sea bed is now giving us great quantities of gas and oil. But perhaps the sea's outstanding contribution to our development as a nation is that it has provided defence against the armed powers of mainland Europe. We have not been invaded for a thousand years.

If the British have relied upon the sea for protection, they have also depended upon it for trade. To support life on these islands we have always needed to buy and sell abroad—even the Phoenicians came to Britain, then on the very edge of the known world, to exchange their cloth for tin. Twelve centuries later, trade in wool was again playing an important part in our economic life. Towns like Ipswich, Lydd, Romney and Dunwich, now no more than a tiny hamlet on a crumbling Suffolk cliff face, were once flourishing ports whose importance was slowly to decline as steel, coal and cotton ushered in a revolution in our economy.

Dependence upon the sea has had a number of side effects. The coastline needed to be defended. The Romans seem to have been the first to realise that raiders might cross the channel. Their fortifications (for example at Reculver, Porchester and Richborough) were known as 'the forts of the Saxon shore' and are well worth visiting. Later, castles built on cliff top, peninsula and island were to provide additional security to many a coastal town. These strongholds were places of safe retreat when danger threatened, as well as defences against invasion. In Tudor times Henry VIII built a series of castle-like gun emplacements along the coast of Sussex and Kent. Martello Towers were erected as part of our defences against Napoleon, and many a block house still remains to remind us of the threat of invasion which hung over the country in the early 1940s.

The first line of defence, however, was always provided by the navy. Alfred built ships to defeat the Danish fleet and subsequent monarchs seem to have learned from his example. Naval and civilian dockyards dot our coastline. Some still build and repair ships, others are more preoccupied with the construction of oil rigs and survey platforms than with cargo boats and passenger liners. Many reminders of our nautical past remain, from HMS *Victory* in Portsmouth Dockyard to SS *Great Britain*, now preserved in Bristol Dockyard. Buckler's Hard in Hampshire retains much of the atmosphere of the days of sail. It was here that the wooden hulks of Nelson and Collingwood were built. Deptford, Chatham, Portsmouth, Devonport, Weymouth, Southampton, Newcastle, and Barrow have not entirely lost their links with an age when ships and the trades which serviced them played a more significant part in our way of life. The homes of the sea captains, ornate customs' house, bonded store and dry dock hark back to times when the rich travelled to the East 'Port out and Starboard home' (posh)—and not by Jumbo jet.

Although our coastline is not lacking in good harbours, rocky outcrop and hidden sandbank have also made it a dangerous one for shipping. The sophistication of modern navigation cannot always prevent disaster—and lighthouse, lightship, lifeboat, helicopter and coastguard station ring the coast to save the lives of those who, through misfortune or foolishness, find the sea too great and their boat too small. The first lighthouse in Britain dates from Roman times. Today they are the responsibility of the 'Corporation of Trinity House of Deptford Strond', London—a body which received its first Royal Charter in 1512, in the reign of Henry VIII.

It would be wrong, however, to evaluate our coastline purely in economic terms. We have managed to preserve some stretches for wild life where, protected against development and industrial pollution, cliff edge, backwater and beach are able to provide sanctuary for animal and man alike.

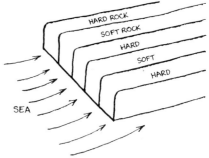

Some rocks wear away fairly easily while harder rocks remain—the action of the sea can have a great effect.

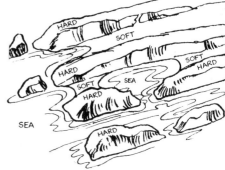

A string of islands is formed after the soft rock that once joined them has been worn away.

The seacoast is an interesting place to explore but beware of cliffs, caves, fog and other hazards. Coastal land has been shaped and changed by great forces inside the earth. At the same time the sea and wind have changed the shape of the land by erosion—gradually wearing parts of it away. On the coast it is possible to see what lies beneath the soil, as here at Esha Ness in the Shetlands, where the sea has made indentations.

These houses on the cliff at Talland Bay, Corwall, are gradually collapsing as the ground is eroded beneath them.

The sea has shaped this treacherous entrance to Lulworth Cove, Dorset.

Strongly jointed rocks are eroded unevenly to produce arches, stacks and caves. This is Merlin's Cave, at Tintagel, Cornwall.

The sea foams under a natural arch near Lulworth Cove, Dorset.

At Boscastle in Cornwall the sea roars through a 'blow hole' in the cliff.

The zig-zag folds in the rocky cliffs at Milook Haven, Cornwall, were caused by enormous pressure millions of years ago.

On the Cobb at Lyme Regis there are fossil impressions in the stone.

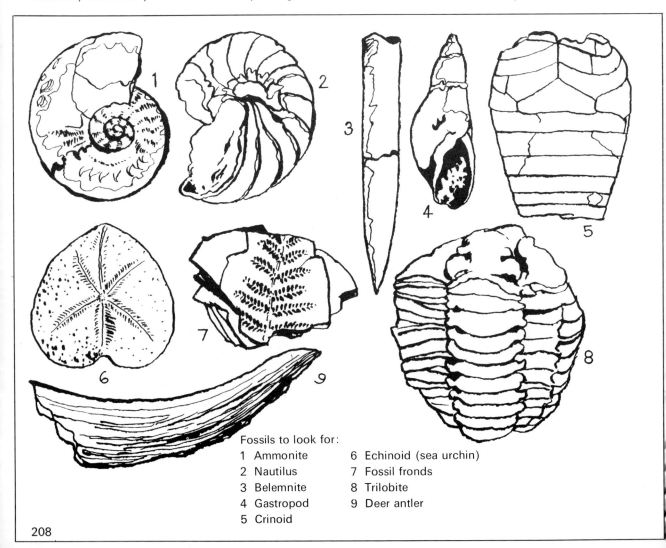

Fossils to look for:

1 Ammonite   6 Echinoid (sea urchin)
2 Nautilus   7 Fossil fronds
3 Belemnite   8 Trilobite
4 Gastropod   9 Deer antler
5 Crinoid

Penally Point at Boscastle in Cornwall has been eroded by the sea to look like the profile of a supine lion.

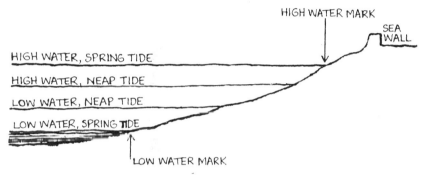

HIGH WATER MARK

SEA WALL

HIGH WATER, SPRING TIDE

HIGH WATER, NEAP TIDE

LOW WATER, NEAP TIDE

LOW WATER, SPRING TIDE

LOW WATER MARK

The tides reach different heights at different times of the year. The table shows the spring and neap tides.

The action of the tides and currents tears away pieces of rock. These are pounded into smaller bits and carried by the sea to be deposited on beaches, sometimes many miles away. Deposits may alter a river's direction at the mouth, form a spit of land or headland or, as here at Chesil Beach, Dorset, create a great bank of shingle.

209

GUARDING THE COAST

The ruins of Tintagel Castle, Cornwall, where King Arthur was supposed to have been born, are on a cliff which rises ninety metres above the sea.

Coastal forts and castles have been built since Roman times. The coast was very important for defence. Bamburgh Castle, Northumberland, towers over the village of Bamburgh.

Southsea Castle in Hampshire is one of Henry VIII's coastal fortifications. It is now a museum. A lighthouse has also been added.

When Britain was threatened by Napoleon's army, a chain of Martello Towers was built. This type of defence had been used against the British in Corsica, on Cape Mortella. It was really a gun platform.

During the centuries following the Norman invasion, a number of ports were developed because they were on that narrow part of the English Channel facing Normandy. These were the Cinque Ports and Two Ancient Towns. Here, at one of the ports, Sandwich, the barbican and gateway stand guard.

A much later, Second World War fort, guards Portsmouth Docks and Southsea.

Guided missile ship.

The drum that Sir Francis Drake took with him on his voyage round the world. When beaten, Drake will return, according to legend, to defeat England's enemies.

Lord Nelson's flagship, the *Victory*, is kept in dry dock at Plymouth and is open to the public. Other coastal towns have maritime museums where much can be seen of British naval history. Naval dockyards are interesting places to visit. Sometimes there are open days during the summer.

The figurehead of HMS *Victory* carries the Royal Arms.

FISHING

Over the past fifty years many fishing ports have declined. Many small businesses still flourish, however, particularly those dealing in winkles crabs and lobsters.

Boats range in size from small inshore boats to quite large trawlers.

Fishermen and fishing ports have a fascination of their own. Each harbour has its own peculiarities. This plaque is from a Seamen's Mission on the north-east coast of Scotland.

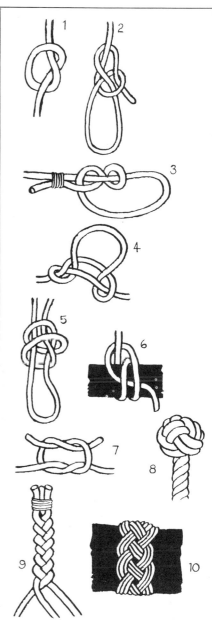

Useful knots for sailors:
1 Overhand knot
2 Bow line
3 Midshipman's hitch
4 Butterfly knot
5 Running knot
6 Fisherman's bend
7 Reef knot
8 Manrope knot
9 Common sennit
10 Turk's head

The day's catch is auctioned at Eyemouth in Scotland.

This fishing boat in Littlehampton Harbour is still powered by sail.

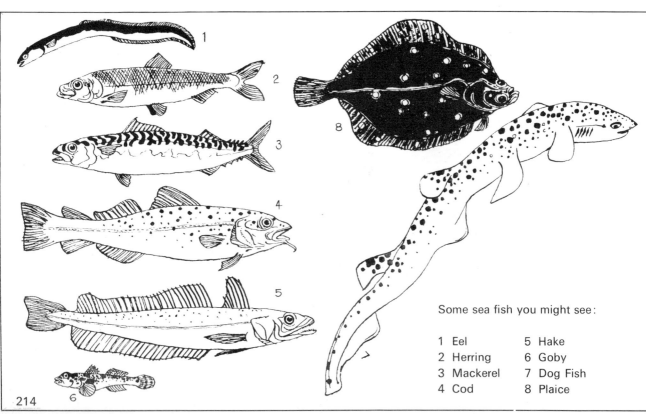

Some sea fish you might see:

1 Eel
2 Herring
3 Mackerel
4 Cod
5 Hake
6 Goby
7 Dog Fish
8 Plaice

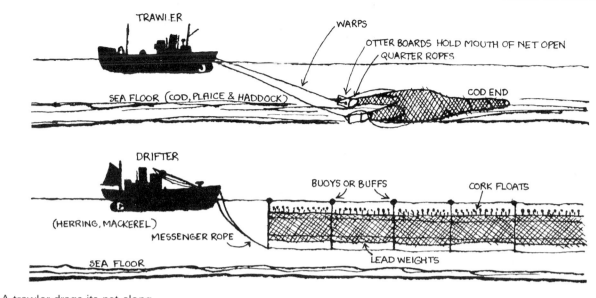

TRAWLER

WARPS

OTTER BOARDS HOLD MOUTH OF NET OPEN

QUARTER ROPES

COD END

SEA FLOOR (COD, PLAICE & HADDOCK)

DRIFTER

BUOYS OR BUFFS

CORK FLOATS

(HERRING, MACKEREL)

MESSENGER ROPE

LEAD WEIGHTS

SEA FLOOR

A trawler drags its net along the sea floor; a drifter lets the net float while drifting.

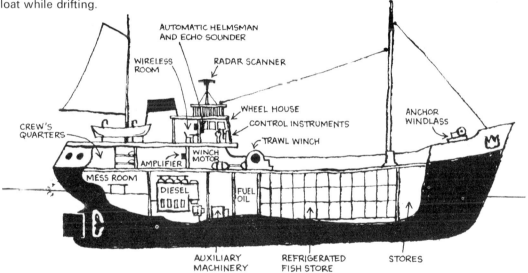

AUTOMATIC HELMSMAN AND ECHO SOUNDER

WIRELESS ROOM

RADAR SCANNER

WHEEL HOUSE

CONTROL INSTRUMENTS

ANCHOR WINDLASS

CREW'S QUARTERS

TRAWL WINCH

AMPLIFIER

WINCH MOTOR

MESS ROOM

DIESEL

FUEL OIL

AUXILIARY MACHINERY

REFRIGERATED FISH STORE

STORES

A sectional view of a trawler.

An inclined ramp, called a platt, makes it easier to moor and launch boats, at Port Isaac in Cornwall. Boats can be wheeled down to the water until they float free.

SHIPS & BOATS

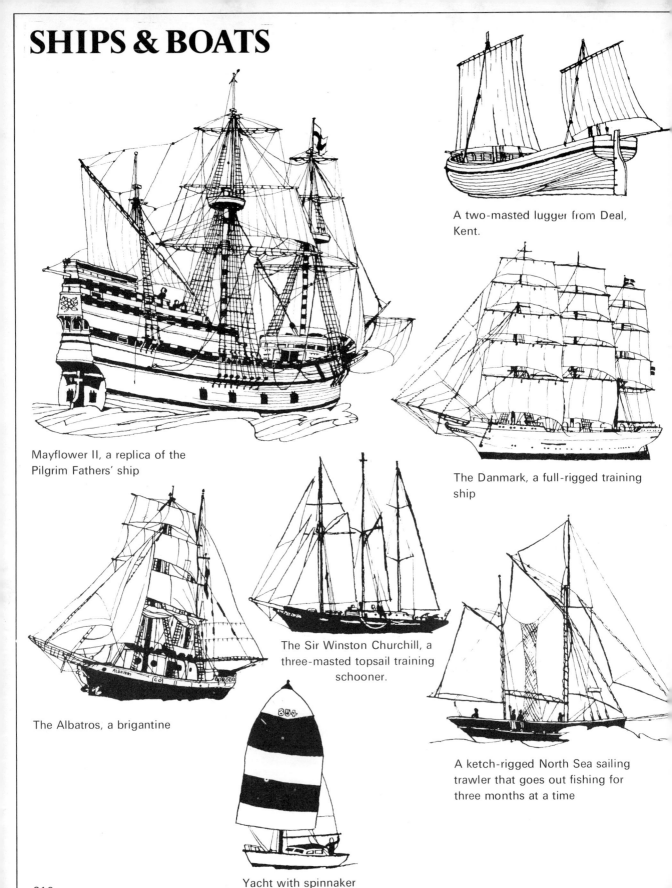

Mayflower II, a replica of the
Pilgrim Fathers' ship

A two-masted lugger from Deal,
Kent.

The Danmark, a full-rigged training
ship

The Albatros, a brigantine

The Sir Winston Churchill, a
three-masted topsail training
schooner.

A ketch-rigged North Sea sailing
trawler that goes out fishing for
three months at a time

Yacht with spinnaker

Submarine

Aircraft carrier

Tug

Motor Tanker

Steam Coaster

Container Ship

Hovercraft

Hydroplane

Passenger liner

217

LIFESAVING

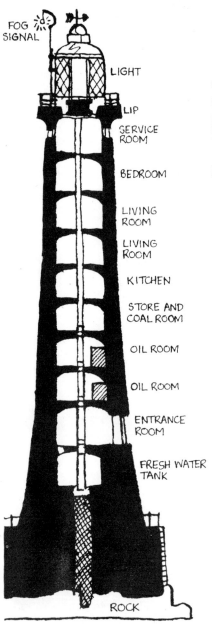

- FOG SIGNAL
- LIGHT
- LIP
- SERVICE ROOM
- BEDROOM
- LIVING ROOM
- LIVING ROOM
- KITCHEN
- STORE AND COAL ROOM
- OIL ROOM
- OIL ROOM
- ENTRANCE ROOM
- FRESH WATER TANK
- ROCK

Britain is surrounded by lighthouses and lightvessels. There are nearly a hundred to warn seamen of the presence of rocks or a dangerous headland. This cross-section is of a tower lighthouse.

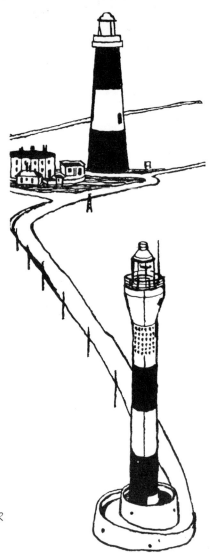

At Dungeness the land is being built up by the sea. So a new lighthouse had to be built nearer the sea.

The coastguards are concerned with saving life at sea and along the coastline. This is a modern coastguard lookout tower at Selsey, Sussex. From a lookout, coastguards direct rescue operations using powerful binoculars and VHF radio.

There are many lifeboat stations. Here lifeboatmen go to the rescue at Kilcobben Cove in Cornwall.

Coastal museums contain interesting items from wrecks. This is a figurehead from the Mary Hay, wrecked off the Scillies.

Lightvessels are used in places where a lighthouse cannot be built.

A steep ramp at Selsey lifeboat station, Sussex, provides the means for a fast start to a rescue launch. Tractors are sometimes used for towing lifeboats into the sea where there is no slipway.

COASTAL INDUSTRY

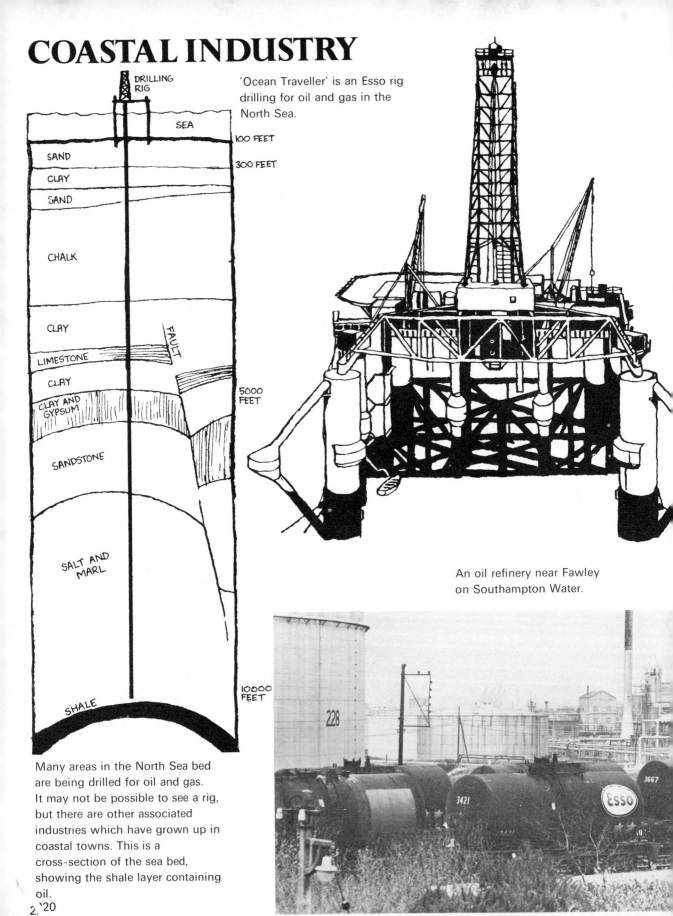

DRILLING RIG

SEA

100 FEET

300 FEET

SAND

CLAY

SAND

CHALK

CLAY

FAULT

LIMESTONE

CLAY

CLAY AND GYPSUM

5000 FEET

SANDSTONE

SALT AND MARL

10000 FEET

SHALE

'Ocean Traveller' is an Esso rig drilling for oil and gas in the North Sea.

An oil refinery near Fawley on Southampton Water.

Many areas in the North Sea bed are being drilled for oil and gas. It may not be possible to see a rig, but there are other associated industries which have grown up in coastal towns. This is a cross-section of the sea bed, showing the shale layer containing oil.

2. '20

Nuclear power stations need a huge water source so are usually built on the coast. This atomic power station is on Southampton Water.

Ship building is an important coastal industry. Here an engine is being installed on Tyneside.

Radar stations and sophisticated electronic devices dot the coastline. The Goonhilly Down aerial in Cornwall has a diameter of 25 metres.

SEASIDE

The 'Blue Peter' is the international code signal flag for 'P'. It means the ship is about to leave harbour.

PHOTOGRAPH ALBUM

Wish you were here

1900

1910

1920

1970

In the twentieth century beachwear has undergone many changes.

Donkey rides on the beach.

A promenade shelter at Weston-super-Mare, with attractive ironwork, dates from 1905.

Groynes were built to ensure that the beaches do not drift Eastwards with the tides. This is at Bognor Regis, Sussex.

x

222

The pavilion on
Weston-super-Mare's 'Grand Pier'
provides entertainment.

The Grand Hotel, Brighton, Sussex,
is an elaborate example of Regency
architecture.

A fishing boat weathervane tops a
promenade shelter in
Weston-super-Mare.

'Shell House' in Polperro, Cornwall.

Built by Brunel in 1843, the SS *Great Britain* is shown undergoing restoration in Bristol.

Sir Francis Chichester in *Gipsy Moth* III.

The statue of William, Prince of Orange, afterwards King of Great Britain and Ireland, was erected at Brixham Harbour, Devon, near the spot where he landed in 1688.

The Mermaid Inn in Rye Sussex, was once a favourite haunt of smugglers.

The Marine Parade at Lyme Regis, Dorset, is the setting used by Jane Austen for an episode in the novel *Persuasion*.